THE

# ALLOTMENT COOKBOOK

The fruit and vegetable grower's recipe guide

KATHRYN HAWKINS

NEW
HOLLAND

# CONTENTS

## RECIPES **96**

# INTRODUCTION

I come from a family of gardeners. My maternal grandfather was a great gardener and used to provide a wide array of home-grown produce from his back garden and from an additional allotment near his home in South Devon. His runner beans and carrots are the tastiest I've eaten to this day. Granny used to make lusciously fragrant raspberry jam, and the sweet, pink rhubarb went into pie fillings or was simply stewed to be served with thick creamy custard or clotted cream. Mum is her 'father's daughter' and has carried on the tradition since her retirement by growing a selection of produce, and my brother has made a career out of gardening! For my part, since I moved out of an overpopulated part of south London to the wide open spaces of Perthshire in Scotland, I've started growing raspberries, loganberries, strawberries and apples, and of course, the obligatory herbs. As I get more settled, I plan to start growing vegetables with the hope of rivalling my grand-dad's beans!

Growing your own produce means different things to different people. To me it means the best flavoured fruit and vegetables you'll ever taste and fresh food that hasn't been transported halfway across the world to get on to my plate. As consumers, we've become more environmentally aware in recent years and subsequently increasingly demanding. More of us are realising that we have to do some DIY in the garden department if we want to achieve a few goals. We haven't all got our own outside space, so more of us are turning to renting a plot. Gone are the days when allotment gardening was a pursuit for elderly retired folk, nowadays allotments are overrun with all generations, everyone mucking in and swapping tips, seeds, plants, recipes and advice. At my mum's church, the minister's teenage son has his own allotment and frequently shares excess produce with the congregation at church suppers and luncheons; he is the talk of the parish!

Allotment gardening is a great way to socialise and an activity the whole family can enjoy. There's nothing healthy about sitting in front of a computer or TV, but getting the kids involved in a family outdoor activity can be difficult. Showing them how fruit and vegetables grow and encouraging them to look after the plants and finally reap the rewards is an excellent way to introduce new foods in the diet and encourage healthy eating and an interest in nutrition without them realising, and it's good exercise to boot. Remember that this is the generation of children of whom many think a chip comes out of a bag from the freezer, and not from a vegetable that grows in the ground! It is a sobering thought and should be enough to convince anyone contemplating growing their own.

Once you've got things up and running, you'll get your first harvest and then find you've got more produce than you know what to do with. Apart from showering friends and family with the fruits of your labours, this is the guide you'll be able to turn to for inspirational ideas to make the most of what you've grown and hopefully enable you to enjoy your home-grown produce all year round. The front of the book features an A–Z guide through the fruit and vegetables you are most likely to grow and gives quick recipe tips to inspire you. The second half of the book concentrates on more detailed recipes for everyday use, entertaining family and friends and for preserving produce for longer storage. I hope you find the book useful. It has been a joy to compile and an inspiration, turning my mostly floury fingers green! Happy gardening and cooking!

Kathryn

# FRUIT AND VEGETABLE GLOSSARY

# APPLES

Probably the most well known and much loved of all fruit, apples grow wherever there is sun, the right balance of rain and a cooler temperature to help them develop the perfect taste, texture and colour. Originally, apple trees grew wild in Europe and the near East, and were first cultivated by the Romans. There are over 700 varieties from those with soft, sweet flesh ready for eating off the tree through to the crisp and sour, more ideally suited to cooking and sweetening. The earliest apples are ready for picking and eating in August, and the later ones can be stored right through until the following spring.

## VARIETIES

### EARLY APPLES

**Discovery**  Pick and eat mid to end of August. Crisp, sweet and juicy flesh with bright red skin.

**George Cave**  Pick and eat in August. Sweet, fragrant flavour. Bright red skin with yellowing patches.

**Grenadier**  Ready to pick and cook between August and September. Firm flesh with an acid flavour. Greenish yellow skin.

### MID-SEASON APPLES

**Cox's Orange Pippin**  Ready to pick in early October, best eaten before end of December. Dull yellowish green skin and pale red stripes or flashes. The skin is very aromatic and should be eaten for a fuller flavour. The flesh is yellowish and crisp with a good balance of sweet and acid. Cooks well and retains shape.

**Egremont Russet**  Pick late September, best eaten by end of December. Unusual matt golden brown skin, with hard, white flesh and nutty flavour. Good with cheese and cooks well in pies and other baked apple dishes.

**Golden Delicious**  Pick in mid-October and use by end of following January. The skin can be pale green to yellow. The flesh is crisp, honey-sweet with no acidity. Cooks well and retains shape.

**Golden Noble**  Pick in late September and will store through to end of following January. An excellent cooking apple with yellowish green skin, tender yellow flesh and acid flavour.

**James Grieve**  Pick in early September and eat by end of October. Yellow and crimson in skin colour with yellowish juicy tender flesh. The flavour is sweet with good balance of acidity. Useful for cooking in summer months. If stored, texture softens but flavour remains strong.

**Laxton's Fortune** Pick in mid-September and eat by end of October. The apple has a sweet, rich flavour, with yellowish green skin and muted red patches.

**Orleans Reinette** Pick in late October and eat through to following February, although may shrivel if stored. Golden russet skin flecked with orange. The flesh is crisp, juicy, sweet and richly flavoured.

**Worcester Pearmain** Pick early September and eat by end of October as it doesn't keep well. The oldest English apple name on record dating back to 1204. Yellowy green and red in colour with crisp white juicy flesh. The flavour is sharp/sweet with a hint of strawberry.

## LATE APPLES

**Idared** Pick mid to end of October and will store through to following April. Bright yellow and red skin. The flesh is white, crisp and juicy, and the flavour mild but sweet with a hint of acidity. Excellent for storage and also cooks well.

**Bramley's Seedling** Pick in early October and will store through to early March. Our best and most widely grown cooking apple, very large and green, sometimes with a pale pinkish blush. Creamy, juicy, acidic flesh. Cooks to a smooth purée.

## HARVESTING AND STORING

An apple is ready to pick when you put the palm of your hand underneath it and then lift and gently twist the apple at the same time: it should easily come away with stalk attached. Fruit for storage should not be over-ripe, bruised or marked with insects or bird damage, and should be handled carefully.

Apples for immediate use are best stored in the fridge for up to two weeks or in a cool, airy place. Apples will deteriorate in warm conditions. They are an ethylene producer which means they produce a gas which will spoil other fruit so they are best stored separately. Apples can give off an odour which may flavour other food, so are best kept away from all other food. Only late season apples will store over winter months, whilst mid season varieties will keep only for a few weeks. When storing, the apples must be in

perfect condition to start with – remember the saying about one bad apple ruining the whole box: it's true! Wrap each apple individually in newspaper or specialist oiled paper (available from horticultural suppliers) and lay in a single layer, paper folds downwards, on aerated shelves or a ventilated box. Keep in a cool, dark place – 7° C (45° F) minimum is ideal – and check regularly. Avoid putting different varieties in the same box.

Apples can also be stored unwrapped in open fibre trays, which look like big egg boxes. These can be purchased from specialists or from your greengrocer. The advantage of this method is that the trays can be stacked on top of each other, saving space, and can be easily inspected for signs of deterioration. Keep as for boxed apples above. You can store apples in plastic bags ventilated with several holes – make the holes before you put the apples in the bag to avoid damaging them! – or loosely tie the top to allow air to circulate. Try to store as flat as possible on ventilated shelves, as above.

## PREPARATION AND BASIC COOKING TECHNIQUES

Apples for eating should be washed and dried just before serving. For other uses, peel, if preferred, then slice out the core using a special tool or quarter and cut out with a small knife. Cut into chunks, wedges or slices depending on purpose, and sprinkle with lemon juice to prevent browning. Cooking apples should be peeled, cored and cut up depending on usage. A little lemon juice sprinkled over will help preserve the colour during cooking.

**Baking** Choose medium-sized cooking apples – wash, dry and carefully slit the skin all the way around the middle of the apples. Remove the cores and stand in an ovenproof dish. Fill with brown sugar, a pinch of spice and a good knob of butter. Pour in a little water to just cover the base of the dish, cover loosely with foil leaving a vent for steam and bake at 200° C (400° F / gas 6) for 45 minutes to 1 hour depending on size, until tender. Serve with custard.

**Stewing** Peel and core cooking apples and cut into chunks. Put in a saucepan with the juice of 1 lemon and a little water (approximately 2 tablespoons for 900 g / 2 lb apples). Bring to the boil, then simmer gently until the apples have softened and thickened to a pulp – cook less or more depending on how much texture you require in the finished dish. To serve hot, stir in sugar and a knob of butter to taste (about 75 g / 2½ oz sugar per 450 g /1 lb apples). To serve cold, add butter and allow to cool before sweetening.

**Purée** Once stewed, cool for 10 minutes then push through a nylon sieve to make a smooth purée.

## CLASSIC APPLE SAUCE
### Serves 6–8 as an accompaniment
(about 350 g / 12½ oz weight)
- 500 g (1 lb 2 oz) cooking apples with a floury texture, such as Bramley
- 2 Tbsp freshly squeezed lemon juice
- 30 g (1 oz) unsalted butter
- 3–4 Tbsp caster sugar

Peel, core and chop the apples. Place in a saucepan and toss in the lemon juice. Heat gently until steaming, then cover and simmer for about 5 minutes until soft and collapsed. Remove from the heat and beat with a wooden spoon until smooth; for an ultra-smooth texture, push through a nylon sieve. Stir in the butter and add sugar to taste. Serve hot or cold as a traditional accompaniment to roast pork, goose or duck, or use as a fruity base for a pie or tart.

## FREEZING
**Preparation** Peel, core and slice. Put in cold water to which you have added 1 Tbsp salt to every 1.2 l (40 fl oz) cold water – this helps prevent discolouration. Then freeze in any of the following ways:
- **Without sugar** Rinse in cold water, then blanch in boiling water for 30 seconds, drain well and cool. Open freeze on lined trays until frozen, then pack into freezer bags or containers. Keep for up to 12 months. Can be used straight from the freezer in pies, compotes, etc.

• **Stewed with sugar** As above. Cool and pack into freezer containers. Keep for up to 12 months. Defrost in the refrigerator overnight and use in strudels, pies, puddings, sauces, etc.

• **Purée** As above. Cool and pack into freezer containers or ice cube trays. Keep for up to 12 months. Defrost in the refrigerator overnight and use for apple sauce, as baby food or in desserts.

## TOP RECIPE TIPS FOR APPLES

- Stir slightly sweetened apple purée into a tomato, pumpkin or carrot soup for extra thickness and a little sweet edge.
- Toss shavings of tart eating apples or milder varieties of cooking apple into a salad of bitter leaves, smoked crisply cooked bacon, then dress with a wholegrain mustard, apple juice and honey vinaigrette.
- Stuff whole cooking apples ready for baking with small chunks of marzipan and small dried fruits.
- Grate well flavoured unpeeled apple flesh (Cox's Orange Pippin is ideal) into muesli just before serving for natural sweetness and added fibre.
- Peel and thinly slice tart eating apples and use as a sandwich filling sprinkled with crunchy demerara sugar and a pinch of spice. For a savoury filling omit the sugar and add smoked mackerel pâté and some watercress.
- For Russets or Cox's, peel, core and cut into chunks. Mix with sliced celery and pieces of Stilton cheese. Use as a filling for squares of puff pastry. Bake and serve warm with cranberry sauce.
- For a children's treat, wash and pat dry small eating apples. Push a wooden stick into the centre of the apples until secure. Dip in melted chocolate and sprinkle with sugar cake decorations. Stand on baking parchment to cool and set. Eat the same day.
- Melt butter until bubbling and stir-fry thick slices of eating or cooking apple until tender and golden. Sprinkle with sugar to taste and serve on wedges of toasted cinnamon bread, allowing the cooking juices to seep into the toast. Dust with nutmeg, cinnamon or mixed spice.
- Bake small whole cored cooking apples round a joint of pork for the last 20 minutes of cooking; they can be filled with redcurrant or bramble jelly, or quince paste, and served instead of apple sauce.
- For an interesting breakfast/brunch dish, fry some apple slices in butter and serve on halves of toasted muffins or crumpets. Top with a slice of freshly cooked black pudding or haggis and some crispy fried bacon.

# ARTICHOKE – Globe artichoke

Easy to grow and stunning to look at, the globe artichoke is a giant thistle and member of the sunflower family. I've always wondered just who it was that woke up one day and decided to have a go at cooking and then eating it! Grown both as a vegetable and part of a decorative addition to the garden, the globe artichoke is renowned for its fine, delicate flavour and is one of the most prized of all vegetables.

## VARIETIES

**Green Globe** Probably the most common variety which produces large green heads of good flavour and juicy texture.

**Purple Globe** As above, but purple coloured. Less hardy and requires extra protection in winter.

**Vert de Laon** A hardy variety that grows very well and produces hearts with an excellent flavour; it has more pointed scales.

**Violetta di Chioggia** Decorative small purple heads; not very hardy.

**Violet 'poivrade' of Provence** Small and purple with an underdeveloped choke. The only variety that can be eaten raw in salads, sprinkled with salt.

## HARVESTING, PREPARATION AND COOKING

Mature plants should produce ripe heads in June or July. Pick the heads, starting with the main one or 'king' head, when they are still green, tightly packed and the leaves are stiff and have a slight bloom. The smaller flower heads which shoot off the main stem should be picked when they are about the size of a chicken's egg and before they begin to open. You will need to use secateurs as the stems are thick and tough, then cut back each stem to about half its original size. They are best used as soon as possible after harvesting, but will keep with stalks in a jug of water – just like a bunch of flowers – in a cool place for several days. After cooking, they will keep for 24 hours in the fridge.

The artichoke head is made up of spiky stiff petals or scales that are closely compressed round a shallow base known as the heart or fond. A thick cluster of silky hair called the choke is embedded in the heart. The edible parts are crescent shaped fleshy bits at the base of each scale, and the heart.

## TO PREPARE A WHOLE ARTICHOKE

1 Trim the stalk level with the base of the head and cut off any damaged outer scales.
2 Slice off the head and trim the points off each scale with scissors. Wash well and stand upside down to drain. Brush all cut surface with lemon juice.

**3** If preferred, remove the choke before cooking by pulling the central scales apart and scraping out the hairy choke with a teaspoon.

**4** Bring a large saucepan of water to the boil and add 1 teaspoon of salt and 2 tablespoons of lemon juice. Add the artichokes and boil, uncovered, for 30 to 40 minutes, depending on size, until tender – they are cooked when a scale can be pulled away easily. Drain well, upside down, and serve hot or cold with melted butter, hollandaise sauce, mayonnaise or lemon vinaigrette.

**Note:** remember to put finger bowls on the table as it can be a messy business pulling off the scales and dipping in the accompaniment!

## TO PREPARE ARTICHOKE HEARTS

**1** Cut 2 lemons in half and squeeze the juice into a bowl. Fill the bowl with cold water and add the lemon halves. Break off the artichoke stalk and remove the tough outer scales from the top and those around the heart.

**2** Continue paring off the remaining scales to expose the pale heart and deep pink inner leaves. Round off the base using a small paring knife, then slice off the tops of the pink leaves and remove the hairy choke with a teaspoon – I find a grapefruit spoon useful for this. Plunge in the lemony water to prevent blackening.

**3** The hearts will cook in salted, lemony boiling water for 10 to 15 minutes until tender.

## FOR BABY ARTICHOKES

**1** Using a sharp knife, slice off 1 cm (½ in) from the tips of the artichokes, and cut the stem 2 cm (¾ in) from the base.

**2** Remove the first 2 layers of scales and peel the skin from the stems. Plunge in lemony water as above.

**3** The artichokes will take about 15 minutes to cook in salted, lemony boiling water. Drain well, upside down.

## FREEZING

Prepare using any of the methods above. For whole prepared artichokes blanch for 6 minutes if small and 8 minutes if large, in lemony water. Drain well, upside down, and cool before packing into freezer bags or rigid containers. Keep for up to 12 months. Cook from frozen in boiling salted water for 5 to 10 minutes, depending on size, until tender. For prepared artichoke hearts, blanch in lemony water for 2 minutes. Drain well and open freeze before packing into freezer bags or containers. Keep for up to 12 months. Cook from frozen in boiling salted water for 8 to 10 minutes until tender.

## TOP RECIPE TIPS FOR ARTICHOKES

- Cooked whole artichokes or hearts are excellent accompanied with the vinegary flavour of capers and chopped gherkins, so an ideal accompaniment is a good dollop of tartare sauce.

- Toss just cooked slices of artichoke heart into a seafood stir-fry.

- Roast blanched whole hearts filled with breadcrumbs, pine nuts, little shallots and freshly grated Parmesan cheese. Drizzle with olive oil and bake at 200° C (400° F / gas 6) for 20 to 25 minutes until golden.

- Tossed freshly cooked artichoke quarters into pasta with a few capers, black olives and fresh tomato sauce (see page 94).

- Stir prepared hearts into a casserole of chicken flavoured with lemon and parsley.

- Stuff whole cooked cold artichokes with crab or lobster and chopped asparagus, and top with a tarragon mayonnaise or vinaigrette.

- Fill a cooked shortcrust pastry case with cooked sliced hearts and a little cooked shallot. Top with a thick white sauce enriched with egg yolks and a light crust of grated gruyère cheese. Bake at 190° C (375° F / gas 5) for 25 to 30 minutes.

- Fill freshly cooked whole cooked artichokes with garlic butter, loads of parsley and serve with toasted French bread 'soldiers'.

- Use cooked sliced hearts as a pizza topping with lots of freshly chopped dill, tuna, capers and olives. You won't need any cheese, just a good drizzle of olive oil. Bake and serve with balsamic vinegar.

- Sauté cooked quartered hearts in butter and olive oil for about 10 minutes until golden and tender. Pour over a little double cream, heat through and serve lightly seasoned, sprinkled with chopped chervil or parsley.

# ARTICHOKE – Jerusalem artichoke

A member of the sunflower family, the name is thought to derive from 'girasole', the Italian for sunflower. An autumn/winter vegetable that's rich in phosphorus and potassium, the potato-like tubers have a sweet, delicate flavour, similar to that of the globe artichoke.

## HARVESTING, PREPARATION AND COOKING

The tubers will be ready for lifting in late October. Once harvested, they don't store for long, so are best dug and eaten as required. They keep well if left in the ground and should last throughout the winter months.

Jerusalem artichokes can be prepared and cooked as for potatoes, but the creamy white flesh discolours quickly, so add lemon juice to the rinsing and cooking water. Scrub under cold running water before peeling thinly with a vegetable knife or potato peeler. The variety Dwarf Sunray doesn't require peeling; some varieties are smooth-skinned such as Fuseau and Gerrard and easy to peel, whilst other varieties are quite knobbly and more difficult to peel.

Cook in boiling salted, lemony water for 20 to 30 minutes depending on size. Drain and serve with melted butter. Par-boiled Jerusalem artichokes can be sautéed in butter, deep fried in hot oil or roasted around the joint as for potatoes. Prepared artichokes also steam well – whole ones will take 35 to 40 minutes, whilst halved or quartered ones will take 25 to 30 minutes.

## FREEZING

Either in 'chip' form or as a purée or mash (see Potato entry, pages 72–75). Not suitable for freezing whole.

## TOP RECIPE TIPS FOR JERUSALEM ARTICHOKES

- Cut into chunks, boil and serve in a rich white sauce topped with crispy fried buttery onions.
- Add a few slices of Jerusalem artichoke to a Classic potato dauphinoise (see page 160).
- Cut into chunks, boil for about 10 minutes, then sauté in foaming butter until golden. Season with salt and pepper and serve with a dash of Tabasco sauce and plenty of chopped parsley.
- Cut into thick slices and boil. Drain thoroughly and return to the saucepan. Toss in finely chopped shallot and a light olive oil vinaigrette. Cover and leave for 10 minutes to absorb the flavour. Serve as a warm salad, sprinkled with chopped tarragon.
- Mash freshly cooked artichokes with a little butter, season lightly and serve as a base for grilled or fried delicate fish, such as plaice or sole. Sprinkle with chopped chervil or dill.

# ASPARAGUS

A highly prized vegetable since Roman times which belongs to the lily family. It has a short cropping season of only six weeks, and being a perennial, it takes up space all year round. However, if you love it as much I do, this is a small price to pay and you should be able to produce fine spears for about 20 years from your plants.

## VARIETIES

**Connover's Colossal** Widely grown since the 19th century with purplish tinged plump large shoots. It is an early variety with a fine flavour.

**Gijnlim** Another early variety which is favoured for its high yield; it has purple tips.

**Lucullus** A late variety with a high yield. The spears are slender and medium-sized.

**Purple Argenteuil** Purple tinged, large shoots of good flavour.

**White Cap** Much lighter in colour with a creamy white tinge, ready early in the season, and has a sweeter flavour.

## HARVESTING, PREPARATION AND COOKING

Don't cut shoots in the first year, and be very sparing in the second; it is really best to wait at least three years. After this time, harvest for six weeks from May to June and allow subsequent spears to develop into ferns; this will allow you to get a full 20 years from the plants.

Harvest the spears when the tips are about 10 cm (4 in) from the soil. Use a specialist cutter or serrated knife and cut the spears just below soil level. If not used immediately, stand the spears in iced water for a few hours, then wrap and refrigerate for a few days, checking occasionally to insure the tips stay fresh, and that the cut ends are not browning – this is an indication that they are drying out. In this way, it is possible to cut a few spears daily when they are just ripe, saving them until you have enough for a meal.

Once the asparagus gets too large, the stems become woody and are not so pleasant to eat.

Rinse each spear, gently taking care not to damage the tips, and trim the woody end from the stem base. Green stems need only rinsing and trimming, but white stems have a bitter hard skin which must be peeled or scraped off, always from the tip downwards. Trim the stalks to roughly the same length.

• **Boiled/steamed** Tie in bundles of 6 to 8 spears with fine string or cotton tape. Stand upright in a pan of lightly salted boiling water, covered, for 5 to 10 minutes, depending on thickness, until the base of the stalk is just tender when pierced with the tip of a sharp knife. Keep the tips above the water level to allow them to cook in the rising steam. Drain and serve hot or cold. If serving cold, cool in cold running water and keep in water until ready to serve.

- **Griddled**. Lightly oil a griddle pan with vegetable oil and heat until very hot. Arrange spears in a single layer on the pan, reduce to a medium heat and cook undisturbed for about 5 minutes. Turn over and cook for a further 5 to 6 minutes until tender and lightly charred.
- **Roasted** Arrange in a single layer on a baking tray or shallow roasting dish. Brush with oil and bake at 200° C (400° F / gas 6) for about 10 to 15 minutes until the stems are tender and the tips are crispy.

## FREEZING

Choose top quality very fresh spears. Blanch for 2 to 4 minutes depending on thickness, drain, cool and pack into rigid containers to avoid damage. Keep for up to 12 months. Cook from frozen into boiling water for about 5 minutes until tender.

For short-term freezing (less than 3 months) the spears can be frozen without blanching first; simply rinse, dry and pack.

## TOP RECIPE TIPS FOR ASPARAGUS

- Serve hot with melted butter or a drizzle of good quality olive oil. Add a squeeze of lemon, some cracked black pepper, and either some crispy fried breadcrumbs or a little grated Parmesan cheese.
- Wrap hot or cold stems in strips of Parma ham and serve with a tarragon vinaigrette.
- In southern France, asparagus spears are eaten to accompany softly boiled eggs – dipped like soldiers. Boiled asparagus spears make an excellent filling for a freshly cooked omelette.
- Drizzle griddled asparagus with a dressing of soy sauce, sweet sherry and grated ginger, and sprinkle with toasted sesame seeds.
- Cool roasted asparagus, then chop and toss into a traditional potato salad.
- Remove crusts from slices of white or brown bread and butter thickly. Place 3 or 4 spears of cold boiled asparagus to one end of a piece of bread and carefully roll up. Press gently to seal, then cut into thin slices and serve as a delicate sandwich.
- Mix short lengths of griddled asparagus with freshly cooked peas, broad beans and sautéed courgette and serve as a bed for roasted or grilled fish or chicken.
- If you've overcooked asparagus, drain well and allow to cool. Chop up roughly and place in a food processor. Blend with mayonnaise, a little spring onion and a handful of chervil or parsley to make a green mayonnaise to serve with fish or chicken.
- Use asparagus cooking water as a stock for risotto and chop up the cooked stalks to add to the rice at the end of cooking. Dress simply with butter and fine shavings of Parmesan cheese.
- Replace the more traditional green beans with lengths of asparagus in a salade Niçoise or toss into a Caesar salad along with some soft boiled quail's eggs.

# AUBERGINE

A member of the deadly nightshade family, the aubergine has been cultivated in Asia since the 5th century. Aubergines are grown in the same way as tomatoes but are much more sensitive to the cold and take longer to grow. They need about 25° to 30° C (77° to 86° F) to ripen properly so can be grown outside in hot summers, but should be started in the greenhouse. Aubergines come in all shapes and sizes and range in colour from deep black, through purple, to pink and white.

## VARIETIES

**Adona** High yielding plant with large, shiny black fruit.

**Black Beauty** Very popular and familiar variety, which yields well and produces large, purple fruit.

**Easter Egg** A modern variety which grows quickly and produces small white fruit.

**Mohican** Another white fruited variety, rounded and compact.

**Moneymaker** Copes well with cooler climates and produces a good flavoured fruit.

**Violetta di Firenze** A beautiful violet coloured version that can be striped pinkish-white. It is a variety sensitive to the cold.

## HARVESTING, PREPARATION AND COOKING

Aubergines are ready for picking when their overall colour deepens and becomes uniform, usually between July and October, depending on growing conditions. Carefully handle the fruits to avoid damaging and bruising, and use scissors to snip them from the stalks. Aubergines will keep in the refrigerator for up to 2 weeks after picking.

Wipe aubergines with a damp cloth and trim off the stalks before cooking. Halve, slice or cube them, depending on the recipe. Place in a colander or large sieve set over a bowl and sprinkle evenly with salt. Leave to drain for 30 minutes to I hour (no longer), then rinse thoroughly and dry with kitchen paper. This process helps tenderise the flesh during cooking. Unsalted aubergines tend to have a slightly bitter flavour and more spongy texture.

• **Frying** Coat prepared slices in flour or leave plain and shallow fry in butter or oil for 2 to 3 minutes on each side. Drain well on kitchen paper.

• **Grilling or baking** Brush prepared slices with oil and either cook under a medium/hot grill or bake in the oven at 200° C (400° F / gas 6) until golden and tender. Drain well on kitchen paper.

• **Roasting** Cut aubergines in half and salt as above. Brush cut side with oil and bake at 200° C (400° F / gas 6) for 35 to 40 minutes until tender.

## FREEZING

Only freeze if in tip top condition and consider that they will only be suitable for stews or baked dishes such as moussaka. Slice or dice and salt as above. Blanch for 2 to 3 minutes, then dry and cool. Open freeze and pack into freezer bags or rigid containers. Store for up to 12 months. Best used from frozen by adding directly to a recipe.

## TOP RECIPE TIPS FOR AUBERGINES

- Mash baked aubergine flesh into a purée and mix with tahini paste, salt, crushed garlic and freshly chopped coriander to make a dip to serve with warm pitta bread.
- Cook cubed aubergine with chopped tomatoes and onion until tender. Allow to cool and mix with canned chickpeas. Season with ground cinnamon, a little sugar, salt and pepper, and serve as a salad dish.
- Dress fried, grilled or baked aubergine slices with a lemon and garlic vinaigrette and plenty of chopped parsley for an interesting starter.
- Cut whole aubergines into thin slices to within 2.5 cm (1 in) of the stem end. Fan out and salt as above. Brush with olive oil and barbecue or grill, turning once, until tender and golden.
- Stuff roasted aubergine halves with couscous or a bulgur wheat salad.
- Fry cubes of aubergine and toss into freshly cooked pasta along with grilled cherry tomatoes and freshly chopped basil. Dress with olive oil and balsamic vinegar.
- Make aubergine crisps – thinly slice and salt baby aubergines or half slices of larger varieties. Brush with oil, spices or herbs, place on a baking tray and bake at 200° C (400° F / gas 6) for 25 to 30 minutes until golden and crisp. Drain briefly on kitchen paper and cool on a wire rack.
- Serve cold slices of grilled, fried or baked aubergine with Greek yoghurt, freshly chopped parsley and black olives as a starter with warm pitta bread.
- Roast aubergine halves as above, then hollow out and fill with chopped ham, diced aubergine flesh and a cheese sauce. Top with breadcrumbs and return to the oven. Bake for a further 20 to 25 minutes until golden.
- Layer slices of fried aubergine with cooked minced lamb and tomato sauce. Season with cinnamon and oregano, and bake with an egg-enriched white sauce poured over the top and a sprinkling of grated Parmesan cheese at 180° C (350° F / gas 4) for 35 to 40 minutes until golden and tender.

# BEANS – Broad beans

Believed to have been introduced to Britain by the Romans, broad beans are the most hardy of all beans and are ideal for the allotment. Pick them young and fresh and you can even eat the pods, too! You'll be able to enjoy this flavoursome legume at its best if you grow your own. You can also eat the tops of the plants as an added bonus – they cook up like spinach and have an earthy/beany flavour.

## HARVESTING, PREPARATION AND COOKING

The earliest crops are ready in May. You can start to pick them when the pods are no more than 5 cm (2 in) long and cook them whole. Otherwise, pick the beans as required, feeling the pods to get an idea of the size of the beans within. Ideally the bean should not get beyond 2 cm (¾ in) in diameter for the best flavour and texture.

Young beans, no thicker than 2 cm (¾ in) and no longer than 7 cm (3 in), have the best flavour and texture and are the most delicious. Allow 225–350 g (8–12½ oz) beans in pods per person.

They should be rinsed and cooked in the pods in lightly salted water for 5 to 6 minutes until just tender. Larger beans should be shelled before cooking in boiling salted water for 10 to 12 minutes for smaller beans, and 15 to 20 minutes for larger, more floury textured beans, which are better peeled and mashed.

## FREEZING

Depending on the size of the bean, blanch for 2 to 3 minutes. Drain and cool before packing in bags or rigid containers. Keep for up to 12 months. Cook from frozen in boiling salted water for 5 to 8 minutes.

# BEANS – French (green) beans

An excellent crop to grow as they are ready for picking 2 to 3 weeks earlier than runner beans and are a real treat when picked young. In spite of their name, it appears that the beans originated from Peru, although they have long been loved in France. If you leave the beans on the plant they will mature into flageolet beans which require shelling before cooking, and finally into haricot beans for drying and storing.

## HARVESTING, PREPARATION AND COOKING

The plants will start to crop within 8 weeks of sowing and may produce pods for a couple of months afterwards. The more you pick them, the more they will produce. Pick the beans carefully as you may pull out the whole plant – hold the stem with one hand and pull the pod downwards with the other. The beans wither quite quickly after picking so they must be cooked or preserved as soon as possible. However, you can keep them wrapped in damp paper in the fridge overnight if you don't have the time to freeze them. When ready to cook, simply nip off the stalk end and the tail if preferred, and cook in boiling salted water for 5 to 6 minutes. Young, thin beans cook very well in a steamer for about 5 minutes. Shell flageolet beans and cook as for broad beans – they will take about 15 minutes.

For haricot beans, leave the pods on the plants until they have turned white – this means they are ripe – usually in about September / October. Wait until they are dry, then pull out the whole plants and hang them in a dry, airy place. When the pods feel crisp, shell the beans and spread them out on trays to dry thoroughly. The dried beans need a little soaking before cooking. Place in a pan and cover with cold water. Bring to the boil and cook for 2 minutes. Remove from the heat and stand covered for 1 hour. Drain well and rinse, then cook in a well flavoured stock for 30 to 40 minutes until tender.

## FREEZING

Top and tail, leave small beans whole and cut larger ones into 2.5–5 cm (1–2 in) lengths. Blanch for 2 minutes. Drain and cool, before packing into bags or rigid containers. Keep for up to 12 months. Cook from frozen for 5 to 7 minutes.

# BEANS – Runner (string) beans

These beans are larger and coarser than the French variety but have much more flavour and a juicier texture than any other bean. They are a firm favourite, providing a good crop throughout the summer and into the autumn. The plant looks great, too, with scarlet or white flowers and vine-like greenery.

## HARVESTING, PREPARATION AND COOKING

Pick the beans while they are still tender and young, before the seeds begin to swell in the pods. The more they are picked, the more they will produce. For this reason, large oversized beans are best removed to encourage new growth. Once the beans are picked, any that can't be used straight away can be stored stem end in a jug of water in the fridge for 2 to 3 days.

Rinse the beans well when ready to cook them. Cut off the tops and tails, and trim away any stringy edges. If you have a specialist bean shredder, you'll be able to cut the beans into long, thin shreds, otherwise cut into diagonal slices. Cook in a small amount of salted boiling water for 5 to 7 minutes. Drain well before serving.

## FREEZING

Prepare as above but cut the beans more thickly if you want a firm texture when the beans are cooked. Blanch for 2 minutes, then drain and cool before packing into bags or rigid containers. Keep for up to 12 months. Cook from frozen for about 5 minutes.

## TOP RECIPE TIPS FOR BEANS

- All beans are at their best freshly cooked and drained, and served with a large knob of butter, salt and pepper, and a few freshly chopped herbs sprinkled on top.
- Peel large broad beans and mash with potato – you can also water down with stock and cream to make a hearty soup.
- Mix assorted freshly cooked and cooled beans together with a garlic and lemon vinaigrette. Season well and mix in lots of chopped parsley. Delicious served with crusty French bread.
- Make a humous-style dip using mashed broad beans instead of chickpeas.
- Add mint to the cooking water for small broad beans in their pods to heighten their flavour.
- Dress warm runner beans with a few shakes of balsamic vinegar and a sprinkling of brown sugar.
- Add chopped green beans to frittata or softly cooked scrambled egg. Sprinkle over chopped chives to serve.

# BEETROOT

A colourful and sweet-tasting root vegetable, much loved since Tudor times. There are 2 main types: globe beetroot which are best for eating fresh in the summer and autumn, and the long rooted beetroot which are later and keep better for winter months. Deep red and golden beetroot make a delicious hot or cold vegetable and preserve very well for enjoying later on in the year. The smaller beet leaves make a colourful and lively addition to the salad bowl, and older leaves will cook up like spinach, although most of the red veining will be lost on cooking.

## HARVESTING, PREPARATION AND COOKING

Pull globe beetroot by hand as they are needed. Younger beetroot are tastier and have a better texture; the flesh of older roots can become a little 'woolly'. Once out of the ground, hold at the base of the leaves in one hand and twist off the leaves with the other. If you cut into the root stem at all, it will 'bleed' and the juice stains. Long-rooted beetroot are ready to dig in November – put a fork alongside the row and loosen the soil around so that the beetroot can be more easily pulled out of the ground. Once the leaves have been removed, the roots can be stored in boxes of sand or peat in a frost-free shed or outbuilding.

Beetroot can be eaten raw, grated in fine shreds for salads, but it bleeds on to other ingredients, so it is best prepared at the last minute, and it also dries out quite quickly.

• **Boiling** It is advisable to wear thin latex gloves to prevent staining your hands. Wash the roots well, peel thinly, then grate coarsely. For cooking, carefully rinse the beetroot, taking care not to cut into the skin or bruise it and place in a saucepan, unpeeled. Cover with water and bring to the boil.

Cook for 1 to 2 hours, depending on size. Refresh in cold water, then carefully rub off the skin.

• **Baking** Preheat the oven to 200° C (400° F / gas 6) , rinse and wrap medium-size whole roots individually in foil parcels. Bake for 1 to 1½ hours until they feel tender when squeezed. A tasty accompaniment to duck, game and all rich meats.

## FREEZING

Choose small golf ball-size beetroot and cook in their skins as for boiling above. Drain and cool, rub off the skins and pack into bags. If using larger roots, these are better sliced before freezing. Keep in the freezer for up to 6 months. Defrost for 4 to 6 hours in the fridge before using.

# TOP RECIPE TIPS FOR BEETROOT

- Raw beetroot goes well with orange segments and watercress. Serve with smoked fish and a dollop of horseradish sauce.
- Split baked beetroot into quarters and serve with a dollop of sour cream, a few caraway seeds and some chopped dill.
- Shred beet leaves and stir-fry with garlic and soy sauce.
- Whiz up cooked beetroot and onion in a blender with chilled stock and some sour cream. Serve as a vibrant chilled soup on a hot day.
- Slice cooked beetroot and serve with sliced apple, celery and walnut halves for a wintry Waldorf salad.
- A classic beetroot salad is a Russian salad. Mix cooked diced beetroot with cooked potato and carrot, chopped cucumber and some chopped pickled gherkins. Toss in mayonnaise and serve dressed with hardboiled egg.
- Toss thick slices of cooked beetroot in seasoned flour and fry in butter and olive oil for a few minutes on each side until golden.
- Finely slice peeled raw beetroot and allow to air dry until the surface of the slices no longer exudes juice when touched. Heat vegetable oil to 190° C (375° F) and deep fry small handfuls for a few seconds until crisp. Drain well on kitchen paper and serve warm or cold, sprinkled with sea salt and a little ground cumin.
- Cooked beetroot, sprinkled with a little sugar and vinegar, makes a lovely accompaniment to pickled herring. Serve with chopped dill and some toasted bread as a starter.
- Dice peeled, raw beetroot and place in the bottom of a casserole dish with chopped red onion and garlic. Sprinkle with cumin seeds and a little sugar and vinegar. Use as a bed for slow cooking a leg of lamb. Serve with natural whole milk yoghurt.

# BLACKBERRIES

Often not as popular as other fruits to grow, blackberries are believed by many to be better flavoured if they come wild from the hedgerows. However, there are many hybrids that have resulted after crossing with other berries, like raspberries, and these certainly have good flavour – loganberry, tayberry and boysenberry to name but three. Blackberries will grow anywhere and there are fewer fruits that are so easy to grow. They are one of my personal favourites and I love the time of year when they are in season. The hybrids require the same conditions as raspberries and need sun (see Raspberry entry on pages 79–80 for more detail).

## VARIETIES

**Fantasia** Large shiny black berries that have a good flavour. The stems are very thorny and the season is late August to September.

**Loch Ness** Elongated shiny black berries, with thornless stems. Less flavour but juicy and make good jam.

## HARVESTING, PREPARATION AND COOKING

Blackberries fruit from July to September, according to variety, until the first frost comes when superstition has it that the Devil spits on the berries and they are no longer suitable for picking. The best fruit forms on the previous season's shoots. Pick carefully to avoid bruising. The fruit deteriorates quickly after picking, so it is best used quickly. They will keep, loosely covered, unwashed in the fridge for 1 to 2 days if necessary.

Unlike raspberries, the whole fruit is eaten. When a raspberry is harvested, the white, cone-like central core remains behind on the plant; with the blackberry, it comes away with the rest of the berry. Simply remove any stalks that remain and rinse the fruit carefully before eating

or cooking. Traditionally blackberries are mixed with apples to temper their intense flavour. They make wonderful pies, crumbles and tarts. Blackberry jam, jelly, cordial and vinegar are also excellent ways to preserve their flavour all year round.

## FREEZING

Wash and carefully pat dry as soon as possible after picking. Either pack straight into bags or rigid containers or open freeze on trays for packing later. Keep for up to 12 months. Can be used straight from frozen, but they do hold up quite well once defrosted.

# TOP RECIPE TIPS FOR BLACKBERRIES

- Stir into batters and mixes for muffins, pancakes, cookies and cakes.
- Fresh berries make a juicy topping for cheesecakes and pavlovas.
- Layer yoghurt, crunchy oat breakfast cereal and chopped eating apple with a few blackberries for a healthy, high-fibre pudding.
- Whiz up berries with fresh apple juice and natural yoghurt to make a tasty shake. Sweeten with honey to taste.
- Stew and purée blackberries to make a sharp sauce for game and rich meat, or sweeten to make a sweet sauce for baked apples.
- Toss a few berries into a smoked chicken and warm mushroom salad for an autumnal taste.
- Serve a handful of fresh berries in a wine glass and top up with crème de cassis and a blob of whipped cream, for a quick, rich and very grown-up dessert.
- Pickle in vinegar to make an interesting preserve to serve with cold meats.
- Sandwich a chocolate cake together with cream and blackberry jelly and serve topped with fresh berries and a thick dredging of icing sugar.
- Blackberries cook well in a sweetened omelette mixture in a small pan. Beat eggs with a little double cream and sugar, pour in a buttered pan and add a handful of blackberries. Cook as for an omelette and dust with icing sugar to serve.

# BLUEBERRIES

The native wild bilberry or blaeberry has grown for years in the British Isles, but over the last decade or so, the American 'high bush' blueberry has become popular. A cultivated relative of the wild fruit, the plant produces bigger fruit in greater quantities and is an attractive addition to any allotment or garden. The blueberry plant needs lots of moist, acid soil to flourish. The most common variety grown here is called Bluecrop and it is a pretty and compact plant, so ideal for limited growing space.

## HARVESTING, PREPARATION AND COOKING

Berries should be ready to pick from mid-July to September. Harvest over a few weeks when they are evenly blue and have a slight bloom. You will need to protect the plants from the birds who will otherwise get there before you do! Berries will not ripen after harvest, so avoid any with a green tinge or reddish colour near the stem as this indicates that they are unripe. You'll need to go over each plant several times in order to make sure you harvest all the berries.

As with all berries, eat them as soon after picking as possible. Otherwise, store unwashed in the fridge for 1 to 2 days and wash just before using. They are perfect for eating raw but only take a little light cooking in a minimum amount of liquid if you want to serve them hot.

## FREEZING

Choose ripe, firm fruits. Wash carefully and pat dry. Pack in bags or rigid containers, or spread on trays to open freeze. Keep for up to 12 months. Can be cooked straight from frozen. Blueberries freeze well but do soften slightly on defrosting if wanting to use uncooked.

## TOP RECIPE TIPS FOR BLUEBERRIES

- One of the most beneficial juices or smoothies you can make as blueberries are full of antioxidants. Add apple juice, honey and yoghurt, and blend together.
- Serve freshly picked berries with a dollop of clotted cream, mascarpone or ricotta cheese for a simple dessert – add a sprinkle of crushed biscuits and layer in a glass.
- Blueberries go well with fresh flavoured goat's cheese and would make an interesting starter or light meal served with crusty bread.
- Stir a handful of berries into a cookie dough with white chocolate chips.
- Blend blueberries with pear juice for a pouring sauce to accompany poached pears.

# BROCCOLI

Introduced to Britain from the Mediterranean in the 17th century, there are three main types of broccoli. Sprouting broccoli grows through the winter months and can be eaten late winter to early spring. It consists of clusters of small spears which are cut with a length of stem and cooked in a bunch. As the spears are cut, so more develop over a period of 4 to 6 weeks. Calabrese is a less hardy plant which has one big head and is a summer crop. It has a compact head of white, green or purple firm curds. The variety Romanesco is a very attractive calabrese. It is lime green in colour and the firm flowery heads are pointed. Finally, Perennial or 'nine star' broccoli comes up each year for harvesting in the spring. It grows to a much larger plant that needs supporting and has white heads similar to cauliflowers.

## HARVESTING, PREPARATION AND COOKING

Sprouting broccoli should be cut with 10–15 cm (4–6 in) of stem attached. The remaining plant should be cut back to just above a pair of side shoots in order to encourage fresh spears to grow. Freshly picked spears can be kept in a jug of water, like a bunch of flowers, in the fridge for 2 to 3 days.

Cut the heads of calabrese with about 2.5 cm (1 in) of stalk in late summer/early autumn when the flower buds are green and tightly closed. Once the main head is cut, side shoots will grow and more heads will form.

Perennial varieties should be harvested and used as for calabrese and cauliflower (see page 37).

Wash the spears carefully in cold water, strip off any leaves and trim away any coarseness on the stems. Cook in boiling salted water for 10 to 15 minutes depending on thickness, or steam for 15 to 20 minutes.

## FREEZING

Prepare as above, then blanch for 1 to 2 minutes depending on thickness. Drain and cool, then open freeze on trays before packing into bags or rigid containers. Keep for up to 12 months. Cook from frozen in boiling water for 5 to 8 minutes.

## TOP RECIPE TIPS FOR BROCCOLI

- Dress freshly cooked broccoli spears with fried flaked almonds and melted butter.
- Mash cooked broccoli heads into creamed potato for an accompaniment to steamed fish.
- Cook broccoli and allow to cool. Serve dressed with a vinaigrette flavoured with finely chopped fennel.
- Use small florets as a quiche filling with blue cheese.
- Mix with freshly cooked cauliflower florets and serve with a rich cheese or hollandaise sauce.
- Toss small florets of broccoli into pasta with flaked salmon, lemon rind and a lemony yoghurt sauce.
- Stir-fry thin slices of broccoli with garlic, ginger and red chilli, and dress with dark soy and sweet chilli sauces.
- Blend cooked broccoli with cooked onion, stock and a little cream to make a deliciously green and healthy soup.
- Stir florets of raw broccoli into a chicken casserole for the last 20 minutes of cooking.
- Mash broccoli heads and mix with ricotta and grated Parmesan cheeses to use as a filling for large pasta shells or ravioli.

# BRUSSELS SPROUTS

Believed to be a descendent of the wild cabbage and first grown in Belgium, the Brussels sprout first arrived here in the 18th century. Love it or loathe it, it is one of the most commonly known and grown of all vegetables, and is rich in Vitamin C. The plants will crop during autumn and winter if both early and late varieties are planted.

## HARVESTING, PREPARATION AND COOKING

Pick sprouts when they are small and no bigger than the size of a walnut. The leaves should be tight and firm. The sprouts will then be crisp and sweet. Older, 'cabbagey' sprouts will have little flavour. It is widely believed that the first frost heralds the best time to pick Brussels sprouts as it is said to improve their flavour. Pick sprouts from lower down the stem first. If you cut off the top of the plant – this forms a small cabbage, and can be cooked as such – it will encourage the sprouts to swell. Harvested sprouts can be stored unwrapped in the fridge for 2 to 3 days.

Ideally pick the sprouts just before cooking, trim away any loose outer leaves and slice the base of the stalk. Cut an 'X' in the base of each sprout and rinse in cold water. Cook in a small amount of lightly salted water for 8 to 10 minutes. Cooked sprouts should be slightly chewy when cooked – not soggy and watery like the ones we used to have for school dinners! Drain well and serve.

## FREEZING

Trim as above, but there is no need to put an 'X' in the bottom. Blanch for 1 to 3 minutes depending on size. Drain well and cool. Open freeze on trays before packing into bags or rigid containers. Keep for up to 12 months. Cook from frozen for 5 to 8 minutes.

## TOP RECIPE TIPS FOR BRUSSELS SPROUTS

- Mash cooked sprouts with potato and cooked onion. Chill and form into small patties. Dust with flour and cook in butter for a few minutes on each side until golden.
- Purée cooked sprouts with stock, thick cream and blue cheese to make a rich, wintry soup.
- Serve freshly cooked sprouts tossed with chestnuts, melted butter and freshly grated nutmeg.
- Serve small sprouts in Yorkshire puddings with a little gravy to accompany a roast meal.
- Mix small sprouts into sautéed potatoes and mushrooms to serve with steaks or duck.
- Shred and stir-fry sprouts with leeks and white cabbage. Season with Worcestershire sauce.
- Halve large sprouts before cooking and serve in a creamy onion sauce.

# CABBAGE AND KALE

Not very highly regarded or much loved, the humble cabbage really deserves more praise than it gets. Its reputation for being 'boring' really stems from the fact that it's easily overcooked and spoilt. However, they look magnificent in the garden, and are very hardy and easy to grow, and if cooked correctly, cabbage can be quite delicious. If you do like cabbage, then it's worth planting different varieties so you can have a succession of cabbages all year long, in a variety of colours from white to pale green, to dark green and purple. Kale was once regarded as animal fodder, but nowadays it has taken on a 'trendy' new image and with varieties ranging from the classic tightly curled leaf to tall palm tree-like plants, there is plenty to choose from. It is extremely hardy and will provide a good tasty vegetable throughout winter.

## VARIETIES OF CABBAGE

**Spring**  Bright green, loose-leaved pointed heads that are in season from April to May. Spring greens are the small unformed cabbages of these plants.

**Summer**  Larger compact heads ready in August and September.

**Autumn and Winter**  Have solid heads and are ready from October to February. Red cabbage is a familiar variety often grown for pickling, and the firmly packed White variety is another type of this cabbage.

**Savoy**  Round-headed with crisp, crinkled leaves. A hardy cabbage that crops from September through to the following May.

## HARVESTING, PREPARATION AND COOKING

Cut cabbages when the heads are firm and fleshy. Savoy cabbage is best cut after the first frost – like Brussels sprouts – as the flavour is said to be better. Remove the coarse outer leaves, then cut into quarters and slice out the hard central core and base stump. Rinse thoroughly and drain, shaking to remove excess water. Cut into wedges or shred. Cook in a minimum amount of salted boiling water – use just enough to stop the cabbage sticking to the pan. Cook for 5 to 6 minutes if in shreds, or for about 10 minutes if in wedges. Drain very well. Red cabbage is usually cooked slowly and requires longer cooking (see recipe tips overleaf).

Kale is best cut after the first frosts for a stronger flavour. Cut the centre of each plant first to encourage the production of fresh side shoots. Pull up the kale completely once it starts to flower. Smaller, more tender leaves can be shredded and served raw in winter salads. Strip long leaves from the tough stems and cut away the mid ribs. Rinse thoroughly in cold running water. Boil kale in a minimal amount of lightly salted water for about 10 minutes. Drain well and chop roughly, then heat through with a little melted butter and some garlic. The strong taste makes it perfect for serving with fatty and smoked meats, such as belly pork or gammon.

## FREEZING

Freeze only young, crisp cabbages. Trim and shred, then blanch for 1 minute. Drain and cool. Pack in freezer bags and use within 6 months. Cook from frozen in boiling water for 7 to 8 minutes. Kale is not recommended for freezing.

## TOP RECIPE TIPS FOR CABBAGE AND KALE

- Shred red cabbage and cook slowly with sliced apple, butter, vinegar and brown sugar, covered over a low heat, stirring occasionally, for about 40 minutes.
- Cook shredded Savoy cabbage or kale for 5 minutes. Drain well. Meanwhile, cook onion and streaky bacon in a lidded frying pan until softened. Add the cabbage, mix well, cover and cook for a further 3 minutes to heat through.
- Shred firm white or red cabbage with a little crisp kale and serve raw tossed in a blue cheese mayonnaise, with a little diced apple and some sliced celery.
- Shred green or white cabbage coarsely and mix with a chopped onion. Place in an ovenproof dish. Sprinkle with a little curry powder and drizzle with double cream. Dot with butter, cover and bake at 180° C (350° F / gas 4) for about 30 minutes until tender. Serve with pork or boiled gammon.
- Blanch whole cabbage leaves until just soft. Refresh in cold water and slice out the central core. Fill with a combination of cooked meat or thinly sliced fresh fish and grated vegetables. Wrap up like a parcel and secure with a cocktail stick. Steam for 10 to 15 minutes until tender and cooked through.
- Blanch cabbage leaves and prepare as above. Use to line a loaf tin or terrine dish and fill with a vegetable mousse mixture.
- Shred red cabbage and stir-fry with red onion, sultanas and a pinch of cinnamon until just tenderising. Add redcurrant jelly and Worcestershire sauce and cook for a few minutes longer until cooked to your liking. Good with roast lamb.
- Shred cabbage or kale and add to soups and stews for the last 15 minutes of cooking time.
- Trim a whole cabbage, slice off the top and hollow out the centre. Shred the removed cabbage and mix with a rich and tasty rice stuffing or a buttery breadcrumb and nut stuffing. Pack back into the hollow, replace the lid and wrap in foil. Place in a large saucepan, pour in a little water, bring to the boil, then cover and simmer for about 1½ hours, topping up the water as necessary. Serve with a creamy white sauce.
- Cut green cabbage into thick wedges and steam until tender. Serve in wedges with a fresh tomato sauce (see page 94) poured over.

# CARROT

A much loved and widely grown vegetable that's been around since the days of the ancient Egyptians. It has evolved from an unpleasant tasting white root, through to yellow and purple, but it was in the 16th century that the now familiar orange carrot was cultivated and eaten. Different varieties of shape and colour mean that we can enjoy this colourful vegetable all year round, both raw and cooked.

## HARVESTING, PREPARATION AND COOKING

Early short-rooted carrots will be ready for pulling in June and July – loosen the ground around the carrots with a garden fork if the soil is compacted. Main crop carrots will be ready for harvesting in early October.

To store carrots, remove as much soil as possible and trim off the leaves close to the top of the carrot. Lay the carrots in boxes, between layers of sand and store in an airy, dry, frost-proof shed or outbuilding.

To prepare carrots, trim off the leaves and tapering root end. Scrape small, young carrots under cold running water and peel older carrots thinly using a vegetable peeler. Small carrots can be left whole or halved lengthways for cooking, whilst larger ones should be sliced, diced or cut into batons. Cook in lightly salted boiling water for 5 to 15 minutes depending on size, age and method of preparation. Drain well.

## FREEZING

Small whole scraped carrots freeze well, otherwise prepare older carrots as above. Blanch for 2 to 3 minutes depending on thickness, drain and cool. Either open freeze on trays for later packing, or pack straight away into bags or rigid containers. Keep for up to 12 months. Cook from frozen for 5 minutes in boiling water or add directly to soups and stews.

## TOP RECIPE TIPS FOR CARROTS

- Roast carrots alongside potatoes and parsnips for a colourful addition to a roast dinner.
- Glaze freshly cooked carrots with honey or maple syrup and melted butter before serving.
- Grate fresh carrots with apple, and toss in a lemon and fresh mint vinaigrette dressing.
- Mash carrots and blend to form a purée, then mix in a little cream and a pinch of nutmeg to season.
- Use a vegetable peeler to strip off slices of raw carrot and leave in cold water to curl. They make an attractive addition to salads, or use as a garnish.
- Add mashed carrots to mashed potato and use as an alternative topping to a shepherd's or cottage pie.
- Bake slices of carrot in an ovenproof dish with a little water, a large knob of butter and a couple of bay leaves. Cover and cook for about 30 minutes at 190° C (375° F / gas 5) until tender.
- Mix grated raw carrot with sultanas, toasted sesame seeds and roasted peanuts. Serve with a fresh orange juice vinaigrette.
- Layer grated raw carrot in a small bowl along with layers of other red, orange and yellow vegetables. Place a plate or saucer on top and weigh down for 2 hours in the fridge. Turn out and serve as a very bright and sunny salad dish.
- Boil sliced carrots until tender, then drain well and return to the saucepan. Toss in crushed garlic, olive oil, a squeeze of lemon juice and a pinch of ground cumin, coriander and cinnamon. Mix well, cover and stand for 30 minutes. Serve warm sprinkled with freshly chopped coriander, and with humous and warm pitta bread to accompany.

# CAULIFLOWER

Growing this familiar vegetable can be a real challenge. They need an open, sunny, sheltered position, rich soil and a consistent level of water. However, new hybrid varieties have made growing cauliflowers much easier. Cauliflowers are classified into the seasons they ripen, whilst the flavour is pretty much the same, the colour of the curd can range from bright white to cream, purple, green or orange.

## HARVESTING, PREPARATION AND COOKING

Cut the heads when they are compact and firm. If left too long, the curds begin to separate as the plant begins to flower. Don't cut off all the leaves as they will protect the curd. If you have a number ready at the same time, the heads can be tied and hung upside down in a cool, frost-free shed or outbuilding. Stored like this they will keep for 2 to 3 weeks. Cut cauliflower does not keep well in the fridge, so it is best cut and cooked.

To cook, cut off the outer coarse leaves and the stalk stump. The fine inner green leaves can be cooked with the rest of the cauliflower. If you want to cook the cauliflower whole, rinse well and then cut a cross in the bottom. It will take about 15 minutes to cook in boiling salted water. Alternatively break into florets and cook for 5 to 10 minutes. Adding a little lemon juice to the cooking water helps preserve the white colour.

## FREEZING

Prepare large florets as above. Blanch in lemony water for 3 minutes. Drain and cool. Either open freeze on trays for later packing, or pack straight away into bags or rigid containers. Keep for up to 6 months. Cook from frozen for about 8 minutes in boiling water.

## TOP RECIPE TIPS FOR CAULIFLOWER

- Break up raw curds and shred in a food processor. Toss in a cream-enriched mustard mayonnaise and serve as a salad dish.
- Break up raw curds into small florets and serve as a crudité with a blue cheese dip.
- Traditionally whole cauliflower is served with cheese sauce poured over. Try it with a parsley sauce and some crispy fried bacon on top.
- Cook cauliflower and blend with stock and cooked onion, garlic and ginger. Season with curry powder and serve as a soup with warm naan bread.
- Slightly undercook small florets of cauliflower then stir-fry in hot oil for 4 to 5 minutes. Serve drizzled with a little sesame oil, sprinkled with stir-fried sesame seeds, ginger and garlic.

# CELERIAC AND CELERY

Celeriac is a close relation to celery, but with celery you eat the shoots, whereas with celeriac you eat the huge club root. Celeriac is hardier and less temperamental than celery, although it needs a long growing season. The first roots should be ready to lift in October. Celery needs fertile, well-drained soil but plenty of moisture and organic matter. Celeriac is regarded as a tender winter root vegetable, and celery as a crisp summer salad vegetable, but they are, in fact, interchangeable, because for flavour, they are very similar, and both can be eaten raw or cooked.

There are two ways to grow celery: in rows shielded in trenches, or in a close block of soil (self-blanching) so that the plants shield each other from the light – the ones on the outside should be protected with straw. The latter varieties are less hardy than those for growing in trenches.

## HARVESTING, PREPARATION AND COOKING

For celeriac, leave the roots as long as possible so that they reach their maximum size – unlike a lot of other vegetables, there is no advantage in lifting them early. Use the roots as required during late October and November. Any remaining roots can be stored in damp sand or peat in a cool shed or outbuilding. Indoors, celeriac root will keep in the fridge for up to a week.

For self-blanching celery, start lifting with a fork, piling the straw against those that become exposed; lift all self-blanching celery by the first frost. Trench celery is ready for lifting in late September – the trench is opened from one end and the plants removed using a fork. The soil should then be replaced to protect the remaining plants. If the weather is severe, the plants should be protected further by piling

straw on top of the trench to prevent damage. Freshly picked celery can be kept in a jug of water, like a bunch of flowers, in the fridge for 2 to 3 days; after this time it loses its crispness.

To prepare celeriac, trim off the leaves – these can be used to flavour stocks and soups, or put in a bouquet garni (see page 55). Slice off the root end and scrub under cold running water. The knobbly skin requires quite thick peeling, and as the flesh is exposed, put it in a bowl of water with lemon juice to prevent discolouring and use as soon as possible. Cut into thin strips or coarsely grate for salads. To cook, cut into pieces and boil in salted water for 10 to 15 minutes, depending on size, until tender. Drain and serve.

For celery, trim away the root end of the celery and discard the tough outer stalks. To cook celery, cut in half lengthways, trim off the leaves (these make a pretty garnish or can be tossed into other salad leaves) and rinse well under cold running water. Stalks can also be separated and rinsed separately. Any stringy bits on the stalks should be peeled away. Cook celery in short lengths in a small amount of lightly salted boiling water for about 5 minutes, or steam for 10 minutes. Drain and serve.

## FREEZING

For cooking only, prepare celeriac and celery as for cooking. Celeriac requires no blanching, so pack in rigid containers between layers of freezer sheets, for up to 12 months. Cook from frozen for 8 to 10 minutes. Celery should be blanched in short lenghts for 1 minute. Drain, retaining blanching water, and cool. Pack in rigid containers and cover with blanching water leaving a 1 cm (½ in) gap at top of the container. Thaw and add directly to stews or soups, or cook in boiling blanching water for about 3 to 4 minutes.

## TOP RECIPE TIPS FOR CELERIAC AND CELERY

- Celeriac has a delicate flavour when cooked and if served as a vegetable on its own it needs only a creamy white sauce poured over.
- For a simple salad, dress grated celeriac in a mayonnaise flavoured with lemon juice and French mustard. Sprinkle with chives.
- Add cooked mashed celeriac to mashed potato for serving with fish or chicken.
- Mash cooked celeriac with butter and lemon juice and place in a heatproof dish. Sprinkle with breadcrumbs and grated Parmesan cheese, and dot with butter. Grill for a few minutes until crisp and golden. Serve as a side dish for pork or ham.
- Mix matchstick pieces of celeriac with carrot and leek and stir-fry in vegetable oil. Season with light soy sauce and Chinese five spice powder and serve as a bed for grilled salmon.
- Cooked celery can be served as a vegetable to go with fish and chicken, with cheese or parsley sauce poured over.
- For a light supper dish, blanch short lengths celery stalks for 3 minutes, drain and cool. Wrap in pieces of ham and lay snugly in a gratin dish. Pour over cheese sauce, sprinkle with grated cheese and bake at 190° C (375° F / gas 5) for about 25 minutes until golden and bubbling.
- Strips of celery will liven up a cheese board or crudités platter. The hollow of the stalks can also be filled with cheese, fish or meat pâté and cut into short lengths and served as a canapé.
- Make a tasty savoury soup by cooking celery in chicken stock and blending it up with its cooking water. Strain through a nylon sieve to purée. Combine with cooked onion. Add a little cream and crumble in blue cheese. Serve with toasted walnuts on top.
- For a crunchy winter salad, slice up celery and strips of celeriac. Mix with celery leaves, shredded red cabbage and halved seedless grapes. Serve with a honey and lemon vinaigrette.

# COURGETTE, MARROW AND SUMMER SQUASH

All members of the cucurbit family, courgettes are simply small marrows (although there are special marrow varieties that produce small fruit, so you can get two different crops from the same plant if you let a few mature to full size). Both courgettes and marrows should be eaten fresh as they are very watery and don't store well. Summer squash grow in the same way and for all intents and purposes, can be treated in the same manner in the kitchen. The plants are half hardy and need sunshine and shelter, a good supply of water and nutrients. The trailing stalks and foliage produce lovely flowers before the fruit forms, and they make an attractive addition to any plot.

## VARIETIES

**COURGETTES:**

**Bambino**  Small, tender fruit.

**Jemmer**  Yellow variety.

**Rondo di Nizza**  Round Italian variety.

**MARROW:**

**Long Green Trailing**  Traditional striped fruit.

**SUMMER SQUASH:**

**Sunburst**  Small, yellow flying saucer shape.

**Patty Pan**  Scalloped edge, attractive, small and large varieties.

**Vegetable Spaghetti**  Pale yellow with flesh that looks and cooks like spaghetti.

## HARVESTING, PREPARATION AND COOKING

All fruits can be harvested by cutting them off the stalks with a sharp knife and this will encourage others to form afterwards. For courgettes, cut when the fruits are about 10 cm (4 in) long, usually in about July. Marrows are best eaten in the summer, when about 23–30 cm (9–12 in) long. The skin will yield to gentle pressure when squeezed. A few late marrows can be left until early October, but should be harvested before the frost sets in. If left this long on the plant, these marrows will store for several weeks hung in nets in an airy, frost-free place. Summer squashes should be ready for picking in July.

Courgettes and small squash like patty pan require rinsing and trimming before cooking. They can be sliced or diced and pan fried. If small, halving lengthways is an attractive way to serve them. To boil, cook in a minimum amount of lightly salted boiling water for about 5 to 10 minutes depending on size and thickness. They also steam well and will take only about 5 to 10 minutes – this is good for retaining colour and their delicate flavour. Older marrow should be peeled before cooking, seeds and fibre removed and cut into rings or chunks. The pieces will take about 10 minutes to cook in lightly salted boiling water, or 15 to 20 minutes to steam. Younger marrows don't need peeling, these are good for stuffing either as rings or whole – simply halve lengthways and scoop out the seeds and fibres. Larger varieties of Summer squash, can be prepared as for older marrow.

## FREEZING

Watery vegetables are not very suitable for freezing, but if firm and young the result will be satisfactory. Cut in 1 cm (½ in) thick slices, unpeeled. Blanch for 1 minute, drain and cool, and pack in rigid containers between sheets of freezing paper. Keep for up to 12 months. Partially thaw, then fry in butter. Alternatively, cook the slices in butter before freezing, then thaw completely before reheating in a frying pan for 3 to 4 minutes until piping hot.

## TOP RECIPE TIPS FOR COURGETTE, MARROW AND SUMMER SQUASH

- Grate courgettes coarsely for adding to vegetable and meat stuffings to help keep them moist.
- Baby courgettes can be sliced thinly and served raw in salads with a tarragon vinaigrette dressing.
- Boil, steam or fry marrow pieces and serve with a hot tomato sauce poured over.
- Purée cooked marrow with a little cream and nutmeg; ideal to serve with grilled fish or meat.
- Patty pan make an attractive addition to vegetable or meat skewers for the barbecue. Simply halve and thread.
- Courgette ribbons look great tossed into wide-ribboned pasta or as a wrapping for steamed chicken and fish. Pare off lengthways shreds with a vegetable peeler.
- Courgette flowers can be stuffed with a herb and garlic soft cheese, lightly battered and deep fried.
- Stuff whole hollowed out marrow halves with a traditional minced meat and breadcrumb stuffing. Tie the two halves together and wrap in buttered foil. Place in a roasting tin with a little water and bake at 180° C (350° F / gas 4) for about 1 hour until tender.
- Dip slices of larger courgettes in milk and seasoned flour with a pinch of curry powder, shallow fry in vegetable oil for 2 to 3 minutes until golden. Serve sprinkled with flaked salt.
- Dip slices of small marrow in seasoned flour then a light tempura batter and deep fry to make succulent fritters to dip in soy sauce.

# CUCUMBER AND GHERKINS

A wild plant originating from India that has been cultivated, and now no salad is complete without it. You can grow greenhouse varieties which are longer and smoother skinned, and then hardier, tougher ridged-skin cucumbers that grow outdoors. Gherkins are small cucumbers which are ideal for pickling, but can be used as a vegetable in their own right. Apart from the familiar long, green cucumbers, there are yellowy-green barrel-shaped varieties as well.

## VARIETIES

**CUCUMBER**

**Marketmore**  Ridge-type; good for cooler climates.

**Burpless Tasty Green**  Outdoor variety that is more like a greenhouse cucumber.

**Bush Champion**  Compact variety, good for limited space.

**Crystal lemon**  Round, lemon-like cucumber, with good flavour.

**GHERKIN**

**Fortos**  Good for an even-sized crop, so perfect for pickles.

**Gherkin**  Fast growing, plenty of small prickly fruits.

**Vert Petit de Paris**  Prolific French variety.

## HARVESTING, PREPARATION AND COOKING

If left cucumbers will grow to huge proportions, but the flavour will deteriorate so they are best cut when they reach the recommended size – this depends on the variety – and will usually be from the end of July to the middle of September. As with all watery vegetables, they are best cut and used immediately. Large cucumbers will keep for 2 to 3 days in the fridge, but gherkins start to become rubbery quite quickly, so are best preserved or eaten the day they are picked.

Cucumbers are most usually eaten in salads. Rinse, dry and trim off either end. Peeling is unnecessary unless it is very rough. If the cucumber is particularly seedy, cut in half lengthways, scoop out the seeds, then slice or dice. For cooking, the skin often becomes bitter, so it can be removed before cooking, but it is tempered if the cucumber is blanched in boiling water for 2 minutes. Prepared chunks of cucumber will cook in lightly salted boiling water for about 5 minutes or will steam in about 10 minutes. Gherkins are perfect for pickling, or look great sliced in dainty salads or garnishes.

## FREEZING

Not recommended.

# TOP RECIPE TIPS FOR CUCUMBER AND GHERKINS

- Make a delicious dip by mixing diced cucumber with chopped mild onion, chopped pickled gherkin with whole milk or Greek yoghurt and lots of freshly chopped dill.

- Peel a whole cucumber and remove the seeds. Whiz in a food processor with a little cooled vegetable stock, some fresh mint and natural yoghurt. Pour over ice and either enjoy as a savoury cooling smoothie or as a summery soup.

- Cut cucumber in wafer-thin slices and serve in thinly buttered brown bread with sliced radish and a few chopped chives. Season well and cut into small triangles.

- Add cubes of cucumber to summer punches and cold drinks, such as a dry white wine punch or more traditionally, a Pimms cocktail.

- Cook finely diced cucumber in a little chicken stock until tender, then stir in cream and chopped tarragon. Makes a lovely sauce to serve with fish or chicken.

- Peel a whole cucumber and remove the seeds. Whiz in a food processor with a wedge of sweet melon and a few sprigs of rosemary. Top up with sparkling water for a refreshing drink on a hot day.

- Prick and salt gherkins. Leave overnight, then rinse well. Pack into sterilised jars (see page 189) and pour over a sweet spiced vinegar with a couple of bay leaves.

- Ribbons of cucumber, lightly steamed, make a healthy and attractive base for steamed or poached fish – good if you're watching your weight.

- Bake peeled cucumber in thick slices with butter and mildly fragrant herbs. Cover with foil and cook for about 30 minutes at 190° C (375° F / gas 5).

- Grate fresh cucumber and sprinkle with rice vinegar, a little sugar and light soy sauce. Serve with Japanese pickled ginger as a tasty side dish to go with sushi.

# CURRANTS – Black, red and white

Rich in Vitamin C, the hardy blackcurrant does well in any part of the country. It is easy to grow and lives for a long time. Blackcurrants like to be free standing and are quite bushy, whereas red and white currants can be trained which makes them a better bet if you are short on space, and they are just as easy to grow as the black variety.

## HARVESTING, PREPARATION AND COOKING

Pick blackcurrants when they are fully ripe – this will be about a week after they turn black. The ones at the top of the stems will be the ripest. Red and white currants need picking as soon as they ripen; they spoil quickly and do not keep for long, and will become difficult to pick cleanly if too ripe.

Like all soft fruits, handle currants as little as possible and only rinse just before using. If you are making a purée, then the currants can be cooked on the stalks, otherwise the best way to remove them is by running a fork down the length of the cluster. Carefully rinse the currants in a colander with plenty of cold water and drain well. Currants need little water to cook with, and sugar should be added to taste; blackcurrants are the most acid of the currants and so will require more sugar.

## FREEZING

• **Without sugar** All currants can be frozen as they are, stripped from the stalks, rinsed, dried and packed into rigid containers. They will keep for up to 12 months and can be used from frozen for pies, puddings and jam. Otherwise, they freeze well in small clusters – best open frozen and packed into containers – these defrost well for using as garnishes.

• **With sugar** Layer dry in rigid containers with 115 g (4 oz) sugar per 450 g (1 lb) red or white currants, or 150–175 g (5½–6 oz) for blackcurrants. Use in pies and desserts.

• **Stewed with sugar** Cook the currants in a little water with sugar to taste. Cool and freeze as they are, or strain to make a purée or juice. Pack in bags or rigid containers, or ice cube trays for juice. Thaw and serve hot or cold.

## TOP RECIPE TIPS FOR CURRANTS

• Flavour stewed and cooled blackcurrants with freshly chopped mint – the two flavours go well together.

• Stewed redcurrants can be thickened with cornflour or arrowroot and allowed to cool in a cooked pie crust. Top with a stiff meringue and grill to cook.

• Freshly picked bunches of red and white currants are delicious served with sweetened fromage frais or yoghurt, dipped in straight from the stalk.

• Try mixing redcurrants with other red fruits to make a stunningly bright fruit salad. They also go well with stewed rhubarb.

• The pectin content of currants is high so not only do they make excellent preserves in their own right, redcurrant juice can also be added to other preserves to aid setting.

• For a speedy summer pudding, lightly stew an assortment of currants and add sugar to taste. Allow to cool, then in serving glasses, spoon over sweet bread or slices of Madeira cake. Top with a dollop of whipped cream and chill before serving.

• Stew red currants and sweeten lightly. Allow to cool, then push through a nylon sieve. Mix with sour cream and 'season' with a pinch of nutmeg or cinnamon. Ladle over ice and serve as an unusual starter.

• Lightly brush clusters of red and white currants with beaten egg white and dredge with caster sugar. Set aside to dry and use as a jewelled decoration for desserts and cakes.

• Lightly stew black and red currants together and sweeten lightly. Add a little raspberry vinegar (see page 80) and cooked onion. Serve as a tangy salsa with duck and game meat.

• Tart blackcurrants make an excellent topping for meringues or pavlova with whipped cream and good quality lemon curd.

# FLORENCE FENNEL (FINOCCHIO)

Fennel has a delicate aniseed flavour and is a delicious raw salad or cooked vegetable, but it can be difficult to grow. It heralds from the Mediterranean and therefore needs a temperate or sub-tropical climate. A sheltered sunny plot with well-drained soil, lots of water and nutrients will help your chances of success.

## HARVESTING, PREPARATION AND COOKING

Cut the stumpy bases at the root for use in late summer/early autumn. Trim away the leafy top stems – the leaves can be used as a garnish or chopped up and added to salads and will keep for 2 to 3 days in a jug of water in the fridge. Trim the root base and wash well in cold water. For eating raw, cut in half lengthways, then cut into thin slices. For cooking, cut in half or quarters and cook in a small amount of lightly salted water for 10 to 20 minutes, depending on size, until tender. Drain well.

## FREEZING

Prepare as for cooking and cut into 2.5 cm (1 in) thick pieces. Blanch for 3 minutes, drain, reserving the liquid, and cool. Pack into rigid containers and cover with the blanching water leaving 1 cm (½ in) gap at the top of the container. Keep for up to 6 months. Thaw before cooking and either add pieces to stews or soups or cook in boiling blanching water for about 10 minutes.

## TOP RECIPE TIPS FOR FENNEL

- Cut raw into thin strips and add to coleslaw for a change of flavour.
- The flavour mixes well with fresh orange and is good served with smoked fish or chicken.
- Keep the fennel bulb whole and slice thickly. Blanch for 3 minutes and drain well. Arrange in a shallow roasting tin and top with breadcrumbs, pine nuts and pesto sauce. Drizzle with olive oil and bake at 190° C (375° F / gas 5) for about 20 minutes until golden.
- Add blanched fennel and its cooking water to a tomatoey fish soup or stew and drizzle with Pernod to serve.
- For a simple fennel accompaniment to go with fish or chicken, blanch fennel pieces for 2 minutes, drain well and sauté in butter with lightly crushed coriander seeds.

# GARLIC

Believed to have originated from Asia, garlic has been a staple of Mediterranean cooking for hundreds of years, and has been in Britain since the 16th century. A powerful flavouring with antiseptic, antibiotic and antifungal properties, it is just as at home in the kitchen as in the apothecary. You'll find white, pink and purple varieties, small to gigantic bulbs, and flavours from sweet and mild to very strong. Garlic can be eaten green or dried.

## VARIETIES

**Christo**  Large bulbs with up to 15 cloves.

**Early Wight**  Adapted to suit the British climate on Isle of Wight; it is purple.

**Elephant**  Speaks for itself in size; mild and sweet tasting.

## HARVESTING, PREPARATION AND COOKING

Lift garlic when the foliage turns yellow and starts to die down in late summer – leaving too long in the soil will result in the bulbs drying out too much. Ease the bulbs from the ground by carefully digging round with a fork to avoid damaging. For drying, dry the bulbs thoroughly in the sun and store in a cool, dry place – the kitchen will be too warm and damp. Put aside a few good quality bulbs for replanting the next year.

To describe the flavour of garlic is very difficult. It's much stronger than any onion, more pungent and savoury, but one thing's for sure, the world would be a much less tasty place if we didn't have it! Green garlic (fresh garlic that hasn't been dried) has a delicate, fresh flavour and aroma and can be used as a replacement for dry garlic, onions or leeks in any recipe. To prepare it, simply chop up the bulbs – there is no need to peel or separate the cloves. The stem can also be included to give colour and a more delicate flavour (good for adding raw to salads and savoury juices). Dry garlic needs to be peeled of its papery skin for most dishes. The more you chop up garlic the more flavour comes out. Using a garlic crusher means that you get an intense, pungent flavour in a dish, but a little chopping gives you a full but less intense garlicky hit, whereas peeled whole cloves will impart a mellower flavour. Garlic can be roasted whole in its papery skin – long, slow cooking turns the cloves into a sweet/savoury meltingly tender vegetable, excellent served with rich game and meats.

## FREEZING

Not recommended. Cooked dishes are best frozen without adding garlic at the initial stage, and it is best added to the dish when reheating. The flavour deteriorates after lengthy freezing, and is best used fresh.

# TOP RECIPE TIPS FOR GARLIC

- You can remove the smell of garlic from your hands by sprinkling them with salt, lightly rubbing, then rinsing with cold water before washing with soap and hot water.
- Add whole cloves of garlic to a bottle of oil or vinegar to add flavour to salad dressings.
- Rub the inside of a salad bowl with the cut side of a garlic clove to leave a faint but distinct garlic flavour to season a salad.
- Crush or mince garlic and add to softened butter. Dollop on top of freshly baked jacket potatoes or a creamy mash, and season with plenty of black pepper, chopped parsley and a good squeeze of lemon juice.
- Green garlic makes a delicious soup when stewed in chicken stock and blended in a food processor. Temper the flavour with double cream and stir in grated mature Cheddar cheese to serve.
- For a quick garlic bread, crush or mince garlic and add to a little olive oil. Brush thickly over toasted ciabatta bread and season with coarse salt and freshly ground black pepper.
- Pickle whole cloves in lightly spiced vinegar for later use.
- For a simple garlic dressing/dip, ideal for Middle Eastern dishes, place peeled cloves in a blender or food processor with whole milk natural yoghurt, salt and pepper, lots of parsley, a drizzle of olive oil and a squeeze of lemon. Blend well until smooth and use to dollop over tomatoey aubergines, slow roast lamb or roast beetroot.
- Pot roast a whole chicken with 40 unpeeled cloves garlic, chopped fennel and a bouquet garni (see page 55) for an aromatic, succulent and tempting roast.
- Take care not to overcook garlic at the beginning of a recipe. It can easily over-brown and become acrid to taste. It is better discarded and to start again rather than spoil the flavour of the finished dish. Simply soften over a low heat.

# GOOSEBERRIES

A native plant to northern Europe, but only really enjoyed in Britain. Dating back to Tudor times, recipes for pies, tarts, fools and jellies can be found in abundance. Gooseberries are easy to grow in bush form or trained, and there are several varieties to choose from: sweet to sour in taste; white, yellow, green and red in colour; and different sized berries. Some are more suited to jam and wine making than others.

## VARIETIES

**Careless** Traditional white cooking berries; a mid-season plant that crops well. The flavour of the fruit is excellent.

**Leveller** Yellow dessert berries, suitable for cooking. The berries are large and have good flavour.

**Whinham's Industry** Red dessert variety that also cooks well. The berries are large, sweet and juicy.

## HARVESTING, PREPARATION AND COOKING

Heavy cropping plants should start to be thinned out from May onwards, removing berries from each branch to encourage those left behind to swell further. The unripe picked fruit needn't be wasted as it will still be suitable for jam making. The main harvesting depends on the variety but is usually from June to August. Carefully pick the berries when they are beginning to yield to gentle pressure.

To prepare the fruit for eating or cooking, top and tail (snip off the flower and stalk end) with scissors. Put in a colander and wash carefully by dipping in cold water several times. Drain well and dry berries ready for eating. Cook berries in a small amount of water, covered, for 5 to 6 minutes until soft. If you plan to purée and strain gooseberries, it is unnecessary to top and tail the fruit before cooking.

## FREEZING

• **Without sugar** Prepare as for eating. Freeze on trays, then pack into bags or rigid containers. Keep for up to 12 months. Cook from frozen for use in pies and puddings.

• **With sugar** Prepare as for eating; layer dry in rigid containers with 115 g (4 oz) sugar per 450 g (1 lb) cooking gooseberries. Use in pies and desserts.

• **Stewed with sugar** Cook the gooseberries in a little water with sugar to taste. Cool and freeze as is, or strain to make a purée; pack in bags or rigid containers.

## TOP RECIPE TIPS FOR GOOSEBERRIES

- Stew and cool gooseberries. Layer with ginger cake, custard and cream to make a trifle.
- Traditionally gooseberries are stewed and mixed with custard and cream to make a fool – red gooseberries make a sweeter and pinker pudding.
- Cook green gooseberries until very soft; strain and purée, and add a little sugar to make a sauce to serve with mackerel and other oily fish.
- Chop fresh red gooseberries and season with chopped onion, red pepper, vinegar and sugar to make a sweet and sour relish to serve with grilled pork chops and sausages.
- Gooseberries have a high pectin content which makes them very suitable for jams, jellies and other preserves.
- Green gooseberries go well with musty flavours like elderflowers or dessert wines; nutmeg or lemon juice helps bring out their tartness.
- Eat fresh red gooseberries with soft cheese and a squeeze of lemon.
- Steep red gooseberries in well chilled fruity white wine and serve with a dollop of whipped cream.
- Replace cherries in the French batter pudding clafouti with red gooseberries and serve dusted with vanilla sugar and pouring cream.
- Stir a strained and puréed gooseberry mixture into a gelatine-set cheesecake mix for a deliciously different dessert.

# HERBS

If you're a whiz in the kitchen as well as in the allotment or garden, then you'll certainly have made room for a herb patch. Herbs are very adaptable and will usually thrive wherever they are planted, but ideally they like a sunny position in well-drained soil and plenty of watering. Some herbs like mint are invasive and will spread like wild fire round your plot, so think about containing some herbs in terracotta pots or such like. Choosing which ones to grow will depend on your culinary repertoire, but those listed below are the most commonly grown and used.

**Basil** A staple herb for Italian cooking with a sweet peppery flavour and soft leaves that make it a good addition to a salad bowl. There are two varieties: sweet and bush. Neither is hardy and both require frequent watering. Basil is not suitable for drying or freezing on its own. It is best made into a sauce such as pesto (see page 55) or tomato. Basil attracts bees, so it is a good idea to put near plants that require pollinating.

**Bay** Sweet bay or bay laurel has aromatic leaves that can be used fresh or dried, in sweet or savoury dishes – try adding to milk puddings, custards and sweet fruit syrups. Native to the Mediterranean region, it is pretty hardy when grown as a shrub but needs protecting from frosts and strong, cold wind. It is best contained and pruned as it will grow very large – up to 6 m (20 ft). Once established, the evergreen leaves can be picked at any time of the year.

**Chervil** A hardy herb with fine feathery leaves and a very mild, aniseed sweet flavour. It is traditionally used with fish and chicken dishes, and makes a lovely flourishing garnish, or as a salad ingredient. It can also be frozen (see page 54) for adding to soups, sauces and stocks, but the leaves are too fine to be dried. Cut or pick the leaves 6 to 8 weeks after sowing.

**Chives** Fine tubular leaves with a mild oniony flavour and lovely pink tufty flowers which make an eye-catching and tasty addition to salads or as a garnish. The herb is hardy and needs little attention, but will spread if not contained in small clumps. Chopped chives cook well so adding to breads and scones will ensure a rich oniony flavour. Cut chives as close to the ground as possible and cut each clump in turn to encourage new leaves to grow. Chives don't dry well, but do freeze (see page 54).

**Coriander** A hardy annual herb that can be used for its leaves and seeds. As the fruits mature they become spicy and emit an aroma that is a good indication that they are ready for picking. The delicate ferny leaves are sweet and delicately flavoured and are used in Indian, Middle Eastern and Oriental cooking, and also make a lovely salad leaf. Coriander does require sunshine but is otherwise easy to grow, although you do need to grow a fair bit to get a good yield of leaves or seeds. The seeds are ready for harvesting in late summer, and should be cut off in the seed head and either dried in the sun or indoors. The seeds can then be shaken out of the heads and stored in airtight containers for grinding and using in sweet and savoury cooking.

**Dill** A hardy annual with a mild aniseed flavour, traditionally used with fish. The seeds can also be harvested for using during winter months. The fine feathery leaves will be ready for picking about 8 weeks after sowing. They can be dried or frozen before the flowers form. For seeds, leave the plants from the earliest sowing and pick the heads when they turn brown (usually in September). Treat as for coriander seeds.

**Horseradish** Grown for its roots, horseradish is easy to grow but spreads if not maintained – the roots are deep and tough and even a small piece left in the soil will grow into a new plant. Grow in a sunny or partially shaded area of the garden where the soil is well drained. Large roots can be harvested from late summer to September by carefully digging around the root to avoid splitting and leaving fragments behind. Roots can be stored in sand in a cool, dry place for winter use. Once pulled, store whole in the fridge, wrapped in a damp cloth for up to 2 weeks. Use horseradish as soon as it is prepared as it loses its flavour and discolours quickly – this also happens on cooking. Peel and grate – best done using a food processor as the juices are very pungent – and use raw to liven up dressings, sauces and salads. Excess grated root is best well sealed in freezer bags and frozen for up to 6 months.

**Lavender** As well as emitting a heavenly fragrance, lavender is a useful herb to grow for culinary and household use. It needs a sunny open site with well-drained soil. The flowers (buds) are dried and used to flavour jams, vinegars and fragrant meat dishes – they make a good addition to a dried herb and salt rub for barbecues (see page 55). Dried flowers can also be bundled or put in sachets to scent clothes and protect linen from moths. Gather the flowers just before they open for best results and dry as described on page 54.

**Marjoram** Sweet marjoram has aromatic leaves and flowers which are used to flavour a wide variety of dishes. It is half hardy and has a finer flavour than the hardier 'pot' variety. The leaves are quite soft and widely used in Italian cookery, going especially well with tomatoes and fish. The leaves are ready for harvesting from May to September, and the flowers from June onwards. Neither dries well but the leaves will freeze – best before flowering.

**Mint** There are many different varieties to grow from the exotic pineapple and ginger to the common spearmint and peppermint. Leaves not only vary in flavour but also in size, colour and texture, so the choice is a personal one. Spearmint and apple mint will cater for most culinary requirements, the latter having a milder flavour. Traditionally made into a sauce to serve with roast lamb (see page 55), the leaves are often used as garnishes and as a flavouring for cooking vegetables such as peas, beans and new potatoes. Pick fresh green leaves in May until early autumn. Mint will dry and freeze for winter use.

**Parsley** Widely used as a garnish or 'chopping' herb for sauces, stuffings and salads – the classic Middle Eastern cracked wheat 'tabbouleh' salad has lots of chopped parsley mixed into it. Best grown as an annual, and to ensure a constant supply, make two sowings: in March for summer and autumn, and again in July for winter and spring. Flat-leaved varieties make a better garnish, but the curly leaf variety has more flavour. Cut 1 or 2 sprigs at a time from each plant until well established and remove any stems that are going to seed – this will encourage new growth. From June, sprigs can be dried or frozen.

**Rosemary** A hardy evergreen shrub synonymous with the Mediterranean where it is used both in the kitchen and in medicine. The coarse leaves have a sweet resinous quality, which goes well with lamb, game and other rich meats. Its woody stems make it ideal for pushing into meats and vegetables to flavour during slow cooking. The herb flowers are pale blue/lilac and make a fragrant garnish – try adding to summer punches. Rosemary needs sunshine, a well-drained soil, and protection from cold wind. Pick young leaves and stems for immediate use, although they will keep fresh for a couple of days in a jug of water. The leaves dry and freeze well.

**Sage** Classically a downy soft, grey-green leaved herb, but purple and variegated varieties are also available. Pretty pink flowers can be added to salads or used as a floating garnish for soups. A rich flavoured herb that is usually mixed with onion to accompany pork, goose and other rich meats. It is hardy and evergreen and can be harvested all year round, but the best flavoured leaves are just before the herb flowers. The leaves will dry or freeze, but it is probably better to just pick them when you need them, and they do wilt quite quickly after picking.

**Savory** An old-fashioned herb with a peppery spicy flavour which should be used sparingly to flavour sausage dishes and stuffings, and also the cooking water of peas or beans (like mint). Summer and winter varieties can be grown; the former is better for drying as it has a more refined flavour, whereas the latter is coarser textured. The leaves and shoots should be picked fresh when needed, and can be frozen.

**Tarragon** Soft pointed long leaves with a mild, sweet slightly aniseed flavour, used with fish, chicken and vegetables. Often used in the making of herb vinegars (see page 55). It will grow easily with little attention required. Pick leaves from June to September; they will dry or freeze, but have little flavour, so it is best eaten fresh.

**Thyme** Culinary thyme is native of Mediterranean countries. There are several varieties, but the common and lemon varieties are the most popular. Thyme is excellent for slow cooking and imbues dishes with a fragrant woodiness that goes well with mushrooms, tomatoes, rich meat, fish and chicken – small bunches can be laid on top of roasting foods to penetrate flavour during cooking. It is an evergreen hardy plant that grows well in the sun and a well-drained soil. Pick the sprigs when needed, and the flowers can be used as a garnish or added to salads. Thyme will freeze and dry well.

## STORING HERBS

Most herbs will wilt after cutting. Placing them in water like a bunch of flowers will keep them for an extra hour or so, but for longer-term storage, rinse them in water and shake dry. Place in a plastic bag with air and seal tightly. Keep in the bottom of the fridge for a few days, checking occasionally, until ready to use.

## FREEZING

Herbs have a freezer life of about 6 months after which time the flavour is lost. They are unsuitable for garnishes once thawed, but are fine for cooking used straight from frozen and can be crumbled directly into the cooking pot or mixture. Evergreen herbs are not worth freezing since it is always better to use fresh, and in general, freeze the herbs that you are most likely to use, e.g. chives, parsley, tarragon or dill. Pick fresh, rinse, drain and pat dry. Keep different varieties separate from each other so that there is no transference of flavour. Herbs don't need blanching and they can either be frozen in sprigs, well sealed in small freezer bags, or chopped and packed into ice cube trays – use I tablespoon of chopped herb with I tablespoon of water per cube and wrap well when frozen; these can be added directly to recipes.

## DRYING

Pick herbs for drying when they are at their peak and in the freshest condition, on a dry, warm day. It is best not to rinse herbs prior to drying – you want them to be as dry as possible to start the process. Simply wipe off any soil if necessary. Choose a warm, dry, dark, well-ventilated situation – ideally around 24–26° C (75–80° F). The herbs should be kept out of the light as it will evaporate the oils which give the flavour. Softer leaves should dry in 4 to 5 days, and up to 2 weeks for coarser herbs, or if the temperature is lower.

Hang stems of the same variety in small bunches tied with string – about 10 stems maximum – upside down, with the heads loosely packed in paper bags. Small quantities can be dried spread out on a tightly lined muslin frame, or brown paper punctured with fine holes spread on a wire rack. The herbs are ready when the leaves are paper dry and fragile. Try to pack them in airtight containers without breaking them up too much – this will help preserve their flavour for longer. Dark glass containers are preferable for storage – plastic absorbs aromas, and metal can affect the flavour – and keep in the dark in a dry place.

# TOP HERB RECIPES

## PESTO SAUCE

- 1 garlic clove, peeled and chopped
- 15 g (½ oz) fresh basil
- 100 g (3½ oz) pine nuts, lightly toasted
- 50 g (2 oz) finely grated fresh Parmesan cheese
- 4 Tbsp extra virgin olive oil

Place all the ingredients in a blender or food processor and blend together until smooth and thick. Store in a sealed jar in the refrigerator for up to 10 days.

## SAUCE REMOULADE

A classic herb mayonnaise to serve with fish. Using 6 tablespoons of good quality mayonnaise as a base, add 1 tablespoon each of parsley, chives, chervil and tarragon, along with 2 very finely chopped small pickled gherkins and 1 teaspoon of chopped capers. Season with a few drops of anchovy essence.

## MINT SAUCE

The perfect accompaniment for roast lamb. Mix 3 tablespoons of chopped fresh mint in a glass bowl with 1½ tablespoons of caster sugar. Spoon over 2 tablespoons of boiling water and stir to dissolve the sugar. Allow to cool, then stir in 150 ml (5 fl oz) white wine or clear malt vinegar. Stand for 30 minutes before serving.

## BOUQUET GARNI

A selection of aromatic plants used to flavour stocks, soups and casseroles. They are tied together in a bundle with string to prevent them from dispersing and to be easily discarded before serving. Alternatively a bundle may also be wrapped in muslin. The bundle usually consists of 2 to 3 sprigs of parsley, a sprig of thyme and rosemary, and a bay leaf. Celery leaf and leek are frequently added if available.

## DRIED HERB AND LAVENDER SALT RUB

Mix together 1 teaspoon each of chopped dried rosemary, thyme and lavender flowers in a glass bowl. Crumble in a dried bay leaf and add 1 teaspoon of crushed black peppercorns and 3 tablespoons of coarse sea salt. Mix well and store in a non-corrosive container or dark glass jar for 2 to 3 days before using. Sprinkle over vegetables and meat to season before cooking or barbecuing.

## HERB VINEGARS AND OILS

**Vinegar** Bruise freshly picked leaves and loosely fill sterilised bottles. Pour over warmed but not hot cider or wine vinegar to fill the jar. Seal with a non-corrosive, acid-proof lid. Set on a sunny windowsill and shake daily for about 2 weeks. Test for flavour and either store as it is (remembering the flavour will get stronger) or strain and rebottle. For a much stronger flavour, strain the herb vinegar and rebottle with fresh herbs.

**Oil** Loosely fill a sterilised bottle with freshly picked herbs and fill with warmed safflower, sunflower or mild olive oil. Seal and proceed as for vinegar.

# ONIONS (including shallots, leeks and spring onions)

Probably the most widely used of all vegetables for flavouring and versatility and for most culinary gardeners, growing a sufficient supply to keep up with demand can be quite a challenge! Onions can be grown from seed or sets (immature bulbs ripened during the previous summer). The onion family is extensive and different members vary in size, colour, shape and strength.

**Bulb onions** Brown, yellow, white and red/purple skinned varieties, with differing shapes from bulbous, flattened and elongated, and in size from the very large and mild to small pungent onions for pickling. Different varieties are grown at different times of the year, and some are better for storing than others. Bulb onions grow singly from sets or seed.

**Shallots** Take longer to grow than onions but are planted earlier and are then harvested before the onions are fully mature. They can be grown from set or seed. Shallots have a milder, sweeter flavour than most bulb onions and are used for pickling, raw in salads or as a base for cooking.

**Leeks** An easy to grow crop with hardy varieties for winter and early types for late summer, the latter being tall and slim, whilst the hardy leek can be more stocky in size. The flavour is sweet and mild, and is popular mixed with cheese – shred finely and add to a salad without a strong aftertaste.

**Bunching onions or salad onions** Include the most popular spring onion widely used as a salad vegetable with edible white bulbs and soft green milder tasting tubular leaves. Welsh onions commonly used in Chinese and Japanese cooking, are more hardy coming originally from Siberia! They are like coarse chives with tall hollow stems about the width of a pencil. Finally, the Japanese bunching onion is a more refined hybrid of the Welsh onion and is milder tasting and can be used like a spring onion or cooked like a leek.

## HARVESTING, STORING AND PREPARATION

For main crop onions, when the leaves begin to yellow, bend over the tops to encourage ripening and leave for about 2 weeks. Loosen the soil around the onions with a fork and carefully loosen the bulbs. Depending on the weather, after a further 2 weeks, the onions can be lifted and spread out in a dry warm place to continue ripening – too much wet weather at this stage will determine how long the bulbs can be left before they split and start to spoil. Ripening can take days to weeks depending on variety and storage conditions. Take care not to bruise the onions and keep the withering leaves intact if you want to tie the onions together for bunching and hanging on rope. Otherwise, onions can be put in net bags and hung similarly in a cool, dry place. For cooking, cut off the stalk and root end and peel away the dry, papery outer layers of skin, and any tougher inner layers. Either halve, slice, chop or cut into thick wedges depending on the recipe. Onion is usually fried or mixed directly into a recipe. Large sweet varieties can be stuffed and roasted whole, and smaller ones are peeled and left whole, then pickled.

Shallots are ready to harvest in July and August. When the foliage dies back lift the bulb clusters and dry for a few days as above. Once the foliage has completely died back, split the clumps into individual bulbs and leave to ripen for a few more days. Shallots can then be stored in a net or basket in a cool dry place as above. They can be prepared as for bulb onions.

Leeks can be harvested when they are about 2 cm (¾ in) thick and this will help to extend their season. Carefully ease them out of the soil by loosening the earth around them to avoid breaking them as you pull them out. Leeks can be lifted throughout winter as they are needed; they will continue growing but much more slowly. To clean leeks for cooking, slice off the root, cut off the tops of the leaves and remove any tough or damaged outer leaves. For cooking whole or in large pieces, slice down the stem halfway through and prise open. Rinse under cold running water to flush out any trapped earth. For other preparation, cut completely in half and then rinse in the same way. Shake well to remove excess water before cooking. Boil leeks in a small amount of lightly salted water – 10 to 15 minutes for large or whole pieces, about 5 for small chunks. Drain well and then return to the pan and cook very gently to steam away any remaining water. Alternatively, slice, shred or chop and stir-fry as for onion. Younger, smaller leeks are delicious served shredded and tossed raw into salads.

For bunching onions, early crop spring onions will be ready in the spring, and later crops from June to October. Pull the onions when required in bunches about 15 cm (6 in) high. For cooking, rinse well and pat dry, slice off the root end and remove any damaged outer leaves. Leave whole for salads or serving as a crudité. Slice or chop and add to sauces and stir-fries. Welsh onions are ready for picking in early summer. The shoots can be used as spring onions, whilst the leaves are used like chives; harvest when required. Japanese bunching onions are ready for cutting 6 weeks after a spring planting. They can be pulled out completely with the bulb, snipped to the ground like a chive if using the leaves, or left to develop into a larger onion that resembles a leek, and thus treated as such. They are best picked and used on the same day.

## FREEZING

Usually only frozen for convenience sake because if you have a sufficient supply of fresh it is usually deemed unnecessary. Peel and slice or chop, then wrap well and seal to prevent transmitting odour. Small onions can be peeled and left whole, and require about 3 minutes blanching, cooling and drying, before packing as previous and freezing. Use within 6 months. Small onions can be added to soups and casseroles from frozen, whilst prepared onion is best semi thawed and used as fresh. Leeks should be prepared as above and cut into 2.5 cm (1 in) lengths. Blanch for 2 minutes, cool and dry well. Pack as for onions and use within 6 months. Thaw in the bag and add entire contents to soups and stews – both leeks and prepared onions are quite watery once they have been frozen, so use the thawing liquid in your recipe for extra flavour.

## TOP TIPS FOR ALL ONIONS AND LEEKS

- If your eyes water from the onion fumes, I think the best way is to hold a spoon between your teeth. It looks a bit daft but it seems to work!
- If you prepare a lot of onions and garlic, it is advisable to keep a special chopping board for their preparation so that you don't transfer their flavour to more delicate vegetables.
- Onions can be baked whole like potatoes – red onions and large mild varieties work well for this. Keeping the onion in its skin, wash off any earth and trim away any loose leaves. Wrap snugly in foil and put in a baking dish. Cook quite slowly in the oven at 180° C (350° F / gas 4) for 1½ to 2 hours depending on size until the onion feels tender when gently squeezed. Carefully remove the foil. Serve in the skin with a dollop of butter or cottage cheese and chives and scoop out the flesh. They will be sweet and tender and very delicious.
- After blanching, glaze small onions or shallots in brown sugar and butter for serving with roast meats.
- Finely chop shallot or bunching onions and mix with softened butter. Chill well and serve as a slice on top of grilled or barbecued meats, jacket potatoes or freshly cooked vegetables.
- Roast thick slices of white and red onions in olive oil with a sprinkling of sugar, seasoning and crushed coriander seeds. Serve sprinkled with balsamic vinegar, hot, warm or cold.
- Wrap small whole leeks in slices of ham and bake in a cheese sauce for a tasty supper dish.
- Finely chop bunching onions and mix into egg mayonnaise or grated cheese to add 'bite' to a sandwich filling.
- Halve shallots or small onions and cook until just beginning to soften. Sprinkle a shallow round cake tin with a little butter, chopped sage and sugar and pack the onions neatly and tightly into the base. Top with puff pastry and bake until golden. Serve upside down as an onion 'Tatin' topped with grated cheese and a little balsamic vinegar.
- Dip thick onion rings in milk and seasoned flour and deep fry in hot oil for a few seconds to make crisp onion rings to serve with steaks and sausages.

# PAK CHOI

As well as the more traditional brassica varieties, you might want to consider Oriental brassicas for your plot. Pak choi is probably the most well known and is particularly good value as you can eat the whole plant. It grows fast and can be eaten at any time during its development. The flavour is mildly cabbagy. There are many types, some with thick white stems and coarse leaves – best for braising or shredding and boiling – and those with taller more delicate leaves and greenish stems – good for steaming and stir-frying. Any flowering shoots that form can be eaten raw in salads or steamed with fish.

## HARVESTING, PREPARATION AND STORING

Always pick when the leaves look fresh and healthy. Pak choi is best picked and used immediately as it doesn't store for more than a couple of days in the fridge before it wilts. Either pick off young leaves for salads – simply trim and wash – or wait until mature and cut away the whole plant. Trim off the stalk base, rinse well in cold water to flush out any trapped soil and shake well to remove excess water. The leaves and base can be shredded into slices for stir-frying over a high heat for 2 minutes; if the plants are small they can be steamed or cooked in a little liquid or stock (braised) for about 5 minutes until just tender, or larger pak choi can be halved or quartered and cooked in the same way. Serve with soy sauce, oyster sauce or sliced fresh ginger.

## FREEZING

Not suitable.

See cabbage recipe tips on page 34 for ideas, but pak choi is better suited to light dishes, mild flavours and little cooking.

# PARSNIP

A favourite of the roasting tray, parsnips are one of the most slow growing of crops, as they occupy the ground for almost a year. It is a good idea to share the ground with other crops such as small lettuce or radish which not only help mark out the line of parsnips but are ready before the parsnips need more space to develop. Parsnips need little attention once they have been thinned out, they are hardy and are harvested fresh when other vegetables are scarce. They have a sweet nutty flavour which is great served with roast beef and Yorkshire puddings.

## HARVESTING, STORING AND PREPARATION

Once the leaves die back in autumn, parsnips can be pulled, but the flavour will be better after the first frost. Dig carefully around the roots with a fork to loosen, taking care not to damage them, before you lift them. Parsnips can be left in the ground until needed, but by February, the remaining roots should be lifted before new shoots begin. Parsnips can be stored in trays covered lightly with soil in a cool, dry shed. Prepare for cooking, by cutting off the top and tapering the root. Peel thinly and cut into thick slices. Small parsnips can be left whole or sliced lengthways. If parsnips are very large, cut into pieces and cut out the central 'woody' core. Boil in lightly salted water for 10 to 20 minutes depending on size. Drain and serve with a knob of butter and chopped parsley. For roasting, boil for 5 minutes and cook as for potatoes – they can also be chipped and deep fried as for potatoes, and steamed in the same way.

## FREEZING

Prepare as above and cut into 2.5 cm (1 in) thick pieces. Blanch for 2 minutes, drain, cool and dry. Pack into rigid containers and freeze for up to 12 months. Cook from frozen for about 10 minutes.

## TOP RECIPE TIPS FOR PARSNIPS

- Make a lovely creamy parsnip mash by adding a dash of soured cream, a pinch of nutmeg and a knob of butter. Perfect with roast chicken.
- Boil parsnips in chicken stock until very soft. Blend to a purée with a little cooked apple, brown sugar and onion and add curry powder or paste. Add more stock as required and stir in freshly chopped coriander. Serve as a soupy starter for an Indian meal.
- Boil and mash parsnips, allow to cool and fold into a carrot cake mix instead of grated carrot – in years gone by, parsnips were widely used to sweeten bakes instead of sugar.

# PEACHES AND NECTARINES

If you have a south facing wall or fence in your plot and you live in a warm part of the country, then you will probably have considered growing these succulent most mouth-watering of all stoned fruit. The plants need cosseting which means that they require pruning and training to make sure they grow in a fan shape against a wall or fence. The soil needs to be deep and well drained, and the fruits should be thinned to give a good crop.

## HARVESTING, STORING AND PREPARATION

The fruit is ready for picking when the flesh around the stalk yields to gentle pressure when lightly squeezed. Pick the fruits carefully to prevent bruising, letting them rest in the palm of your hand as you pull them from the tree. They will store for a few days in the fridge, but are best enjoyed as soon as possible, and should be brought back to room temperature before eating so that the juice and flavour develop. For cooked desserts, peaches and nectarines are usually peeled. Dip them in a bowl of boiling water for 1 to 2 minutes to loosen the skins and then into iced water to cool off. Peel the skin downwards in strips using a small knife. If a nectarine is too firm to peel like this, you may prefer to simply peel with a vegetable peeler. Once peeled, they discolour quickly so brush with a little lemon juice to help delay this. Cut peaches and nectarines in half along the indentations of the flesh, twist the halves apart and remove the stone. Poach gently in sugared water or wine for 10 to 15 minutes, and serve hot or cold as a compote. Peaches and nectarines can be made into preserves, chutneys and jams. They make an excellent sorbet or ice cream, as well as fillings for pies, tarts and crumbles. They can also be dried (see page 187).

## FREEZING

Prepare as above for freezing whole or halved. Pack in rigid containers and cover with a heavy sugar syrup with added lemon juice – 450 g (1 lb) sugar per 600 ml (1 pint) water. Thaw overnight in the refrigerator and either use as they are or drain and use as a pie filling. Alternatively, compote and cool or make into a purée with lemon juice and freeze in rigid containers or ice cube trays. Keep frozen peaches and nectarines for up to 12 months.

# TOP RECIPE TIPS FOR PEACHES AND NECTARINES

- Traditionally combined with raspberries to make a 'melba'. Try fresh slices with lightly crushed fresh raspberries or blueberries and a little sugar or maple syrup, served with cream cheese or clotted cream for a simple summer pudding.
- Sprinkle thick slices with butter, sugar and mild curry powder and bake at 180° C (350° F / gas 4) for 15 to 20 minutes until caramelised. Serve with curries or roast pork.
- Stuff fresh halves with a creamy paste of strong tasting blue cheese and serve as a canapé or starter.
- Grill halves sprinkled thickly with demerara sugar, a knob of butter and a pinch of spice until caramelised and serve drizzled with brandy or Marsala wine.
- Poach slices in a light syrup and cool. Spoon over Madeira cake in the bottom of a trifle bowl or individual glasses. Add a good slug of dessert wine and top with vanilla custard and whipped cream. Chill and serve sprinkled with white chocolate and flaked toasted almonds.
- Peel and prick all over with a fork. Place in large wine glass or tumbler and pour over very chilled sparkling wine, champagne or a fruity medium white wine. Serve as a grown up dessert with a drizzle of raspberry or blackberry coulis or purée spooned over at the last minute.
- Cut in half and top with a knob of marzipan and grill for 5 to 6 minutes. Serve warm with pouring cream.
- Chop peach or nectarine into a blender and pour over freshly squeezed orange juice and a couple of scoops of good vanilla ice cream. Whiz for a few seconds until smooth.
- Serve fresh slices with a warm sauce made from melted redcurrant jelly or rose petal jam and a little water. Top with a dollop of crème fraîche.
- Make a salad of wild rocket leaves, fresh basil and crumbled feta cheese, and toss in slices of fresh peach or nectarine and scatter with toasted pine nuts.

# PEARS

Pears need more sun and water than apples. They flower earlier so are best located in a sheltered position in case of a late frost. The soil should be deep and ideally able to retain moisture during dry spells. Pears like to be pruned and can be trained into any shape; they will grow flat against a wall, or even grown in a tub if space is short. Pears are not self fertile, so you must make sure you have two compatible plants that flower at the same time. Different varieties of fruit crop from August through to the end of December, and late flowering pears are better if you live in an area subject to late frosts.

## VARIETIES

**Doyenne du Comice** Much prized for its delicately flavoured, juicy and very sweet flesh with the texture of butter when perfectly ripe. Best eaten as a dessert pear. A late variety, ready for picking in early October for eating from late October to December.

**Conference** A very popular pear in Britain. Long thin tapered shape with rather tough brownish green skin. The flesh has a good fragrant flavour and cooks well. Pick the fruits in September for eating in October and November.

**William's Bon Chrétien** An early variety with a musky flavour. Pick in late August to ripen for eating in September, but only keeps for a short time.

## HARVESTING, STORING AND PREPARATION

Most pears ripen off the tree. Early varieties need cutting from the tree when the fruit is mature but still hard. Mid and late season fruits can be picked when the stalk comes away easily after gently twisting from the tree.

Unlike apples, pears don't need wrapping before storing. Arrange them in a single layer, not touching, on a shelf or tray. As with all produce for storing, they should be in perfect condition. They need frequent checking, and once the fruit begins to soften at the stalk end, bring indoors and store at about 16° C (61° F) for 2 to 3 days to complete the ripening.

Dessert pear varieties need simple washing and patting dry. If the skin is tough, then it is better peeled. Once the flesh is cut it is best eaten quickly before . discolouration sets in, otherwise, brush lightly with lemon juice to keep for a short while. For cooking, peel using a stainless steel knife or vegetable peeler and brush with lemon juice if necessary. Pears for poaching whole should have the blossom end removed but the stalk end left intact – simply scrape the stalk area to remove the skin. Alternatively cut in half and scoop out the core using a teaspoon and pull out the woody strings that run up to the stalk. Whole pears will take about 25 minutes to cook through and halves about 15 minutes.

They can be baked like apples, although they are better cut in half. Use pears in chutneys, jams, pickles and wine making. They can also be dried (see page 187).

## FREEZING

Not recommended for freezing whole as they discolour and are very watery after thawing. Best made into a purée or packed in sugar (see Apple entry on pages 10–13).

## TOP RECIPE TIPS FOR PEARS

- Perfect flavours to go with pears include chocolate, lemon, vanilla, saffron, cinnamon and ginger.
- For a decadent sandwich, toast brioche or other sweet loaf, and fill with freshly sliced pear, a few marshmallows and some plain chocolate chips. Spread thickly on the outside with butter and press into a preheated hot griddle pan for a couple of minutes on each side.
- Blend chopped pear with blueberries and fresh unsweetened pear or apple juice for a sweet and perfumed smoothie.
- Serve perfectly ripe pears with a salty blue cheese crumbled over and a drizzle of mild honey. Sprinkle over toasted walnuts and serve as a lazy starter or light supper, with crusty bread.
- Leaving pears in their skins, cut in half and remove core. Brush with lemon juice, sprinkle with demerara sugar and dot with butter. Place in a small roasting tin and pour in a little wine. Cover and bake at 200° C (400° F / gas 6) for about 30 minutes until tender. Serve hot with a scoop of vanilla ice cream and a drizzle of chocolate sauce.
- Replace grapes on your cheese board with ripe pears – they go well with all cheeses.
- Mix cooking pears with apples in pies and crumbles to give a more fragrant flavour.
- Peel and core cooking pears and bake alongside a ham or pork joint – sprinkle with butter, cinnamon and sugar and baste frequently to prevent drying out – for the last 30 minutes of cooking.
- Mash ripe pear and fold into mashed potato along with a little blue cheese to liven up a mash – great served with chicken or ham.
- Make a chocolate rice pudding or risotto and top with fresh or poached pears and a dollop of mascarpone cheese.

# PEAS, PETITS POIS, MANGE-TOUT, AND SUGAR SNAPS

Considered to be quite a difficult crop to grow, and the plants do take up a lot of space, however, these plants are some of the most rewarding of vegetables to grow – a fresh pea eaten just after picking is deliciously sweet and tastes like nothing else. If you don't have much space, then a couple of rows of an early variety which can be picked at the same time as the first carrots, French beans and turnips is best. You'll then have the room for leeks and cabbages. If you have more space, varieties can be planted to give you a supply from May to October. Remember to water well at the flowering stage to improve the crop. As well as the traditional round garden pea, there are the very small petits pois, flat-podded mange-tout, sweet sugar snaps which are eaten in the pod, and large fat peas for drying. Young pea shoots can also be eaten – toss into a salad for extra pea flavour!

## HARVESTING, STORING AND PREPARATION

When the pods seem to have reached the right length, check them daily to feel if the peas are swelling inside. Aim to pick when well developed but not overly large. For all varieties, carefully pull the pod upwards with one hand whilst holding the stem with the other. Mange-tout and sugar snaps are ready to be picked when you can just see the peas forming in the pod – if you don't catch them at the right time, they will go on to develop into a garden pea and can be harvested and used as such. If insufficient mange-tout or sugar snaps are ready at one time, pick the few that are ripe and keep in the fridge for a few days until others are ready for harvesting. Pick garden peas regularly and eat as fresh as possible.

For full size garden peas and petits pois, prise off the stalk of the pod and carefully prise the pod open. Gently run your thumb up the pod to remove the peas. Boil garden peas in lightly salted boiling water for 10 to 15 minutes – adding 1 teaspoon of sugar will also help to preserve their colour. Petits pois need only blanching in boiling water for 2 minutes and are then best drained and steamed in a covered pan with a little butter for a further 2 to 3 minutes. Top and tail sugar snaps and mange-tout as for French beans. They should not need stringing. Rinse in cold water and cook in lightly salted water for 4 to 5 minutes for sugar snaps and about 3 minutes for mange-tout. Both varieties are also good for stir-fries and can be used whole or sliced on the diagonal. Young garden pea pods can be cooked in butter for about 10 minutes and served as a vegetable in their own right – break the pod at the blossom end and pull away the thin waxy covering. Larger pods can be used to flavour stock for soups and casseroles. Pea shoots require a simple rinse and shake dry before eating. Peas are often bottled and salted to be enjoyed in winter months.

## FREEZING

Garden peas should be shelled, blanched for 1 minute, drained, cooled quickly in cold running water or iced water and dried and then packed into freezer bags. Top and tail mange-tout and sugar snaps; blanch, then cool and pack as for peas. Freeze for up to 12 months. Cook from frozen for 4 to 5 minutes.

## TOP RECIPE TIPS FOR PEAS, PETITS POIS, MANGE-TOUT AND SUGAR SNAPS

- Cook peas with a sprig of fresh mint or rosemary in the water for flavour.
- Mash freshly cooked peas and fold into creamed potato with grated Parmesan cheese or a dollop of good pesto, to serve with roast cod or salmon.
- Lightly cook mange-tout or sugar snaps and cool. Serve in a salad with strawberries, smoked salmon and cucumber.
- Pack a baked shortcrust pastry case with lightly cooked peas and bake with goat's cheese and an egg-enriched white sauce.
- Purée freshly cooked cold peas with cooked chickpeas and flavour with garlic, tahini and olive oil to make a green humous-style dip.
- Toss cooked peas or pieces of mange-tout or sugar snaps into freshly cooked pasta with garlic and herb flavoured soft cheese and a little cream to loosen the mixture for a quick pasta sauce. Serve with grated Parmesan on top.
- Serve freshly cooked peas with artichoke hearts, a little sautéed shallot and some crispy bacon.
- Serve small cups of cold fresh peas on a platter with other baby vegetables and accompany with a fresh garlic mayonnaise. Decorate with pea shoots and flowers.
- Mix pea shoots with tarragon and baby beet leaves and dress lightly with a raspberry vinaigrette to serve with fish.
- Add cooked peas to a savoury cheesy muffin mixture and serve warm with light vegetable soups.

# PEPPERS AND CHILLIES

Usually grown in the hothouse, there are now varieties that will grow outside – like the outdoor tomato plants – but the pepper and chilli do like the sun and hot weather. Both peppers and chillis grow in exactly the same way. Sweet pepper or capsicum and bell peppers are annuals and the easiest to grow. They come in all shapes and sizes and a selection of colours from a creamy white, to green to yellow and orange, through the reds to the darkest purple or black. Chillies are perennial and the fruits are smaller and again vary in colour; the fiery heat depends on the variety – jalapeños are one of the mildest, whilst habanero are unbelievably hot! There are also mini varieties of pepper and chilli for growing in pots – good if you're short on space.

## HARVESTING, STORING AND PREPARATION

Green peppers should be ready to pick outdoors in August. Choose them when they are bright and shiny. Picking will encourage others to grow. If you want yellow or red, leave them on the plants to change colour if applicable to the variety. Peppers and chillies are best picked to use as soon as possible, but will keep in the fridge for a couple of days – chillies tend to wilt and go limp sooner than peppers.

To prepare a pepper, rinse and pat dry. Run the tip of a sharp knife in a neat circle around the stalk, cutting through the flesh, and pull out the stalk. Slice down the middle of the pepper and scoop out the seeds. Slice out the central paler membranes that run down the length of the pepper. The flesh is now ready to slice, dice or leave in halves. For a whole pepper, slice off the top stalk end and a little of the base to enable it to stand flat. Scoop out the seeds and membrane with a spoon. Either cook first or stuff with your chosen filling and replace the top ready for baking. This is also the preparation for ring slices of pepper.

For chillies, the important thing to remember is that the juices can be an irritant to the skin, particularly the hot chilli varieties, so take extra care. I find it easier to wear thin latex gloves to avoid getting any juice on my skin. After rinsing and drying, slice down the length of the chilli and carefully slice out the seeds and membrane by running the tip of a small knife underneath. If the chilli is small and fiddly, it is often easier to gently scrape the seeds and membrane out. Rinse under water to remove any stray seeds and then chop or slice. Rinse hands in cold running water, and wash the knife and board thoroughly as soon as you can after preparing chillies to avoid irritation and transferring the juices on to other foods.

Peppers can be used as salad vegetables and their crunchy texture and spicy flavour add 'bite' to leaves and herbs. Heat lovers can add freshly chopped chilli to dishes for fiery spiciness, but do this in moderation ! Peppers and chillies can be added to cooked dishes and are usually fried with onions and garlic at the beginning of a recipe. Both are also added to chutneys, relishes, sauces and pickles for added pep and spice.

## SKINNING PEPPERS AND CHILLIES

Sometimes a recipe calls for peppers or chillies to be skinned. This is done for marinating purposes or to give a sweeter, more refined finish to a recipe. There are different ways to remove the skin from a pepper or chilli and this is the way that works for me. It is more time consuming removing chilli skin, and I would only bother with the larger milder varieties if you are going to use them whole. Preheat the grill to its hottest setting and prepare the peppers in halves or the chillies left whole (but seeded and stalks removed). Lie skin side up on a grill rack and cook for 3 to 5 minutes (turning chillies halfway through to do the other side) until the skin starts to blacken and blister. Carefully remove from the grill rack and place in a shallow heatproof dish. Immediately lay clear wrap directly on the blistered skin and set aside until cool enough to handle. This helps keep the moisture in the peppers and should enable you to peel away the blistered skin more easily. The skin should peel away in strips as you pull it carefully with your fingers; any stubborn bits that remain can be carefully sliced off using a small sharp knife or vegetable peeler.

## FREEZING

Prepare peppers as described and either cut in halves, slices or dice. Blanch for 1 to 3 minutes depending on size, drain, cool and pat dry. Pack into freezer bags and seal well. Keep for up to 12 months. Thaw halves of pepper for a couple of hours ready for using stuffed, or add slices and chopped peppers directly to soups and stews, or other cooked dishes. If you want to freeze chillies, it is best to chop them first – they won't need blanching – and pack carefully in small bundles, well wrapped and easily identifiable. Store for up to 6 months and use straight from frozen.

# TOP RECIPE TIPS FOR PEPPERS AND CHILLIES

- Lightly blister prepared mild green chillies under a hot grill or on the barbecue. Cool, skin and then stuff with creamy goat's cheese. Either serve as a tasty snack or marinade in olive oil and refrigerate for later use. You can also use this method for stuffing baby peppers, which can then be dipped in batter and deep fried.

- Soften sliced peppers and a little onion in butter in a covered pan until collapsed. Stir into scrambled eggs or an omelette.

- For a hot and spicy oil for dressings and salads, blanch hot chillies for 1 minute, then pat dry. Crush slightly and place in a sterilised bottle. Pour in olive oil and seal. Shake well and stand in a cool, dark place for 2 months before using. Use 4 hot chillies per 1 litre (35 fl oz) oil.

- If you find chillies a bind to prepare, make a paste from a batch of hot chillies. Prepare and blend in a blender or food processor with a little chopped onion, garlic and salt until smooth – take care to avoid inhaling the fumes. Pack into a sterilised jar and top with olive oil to cover. Seal well and store in the fridge. This will keep for weeks providing the paste is covered with oil and the oil is changed every 3 to 4 weeks to keep it fresh.

- For baking a pepper, prepare as described and cook in lightly salted boiling water for 5 minutes. Drain well and cool. Stuff with chosen filling – rice-based, breadcrumb or nut-based, or a chopped meat filling work well – replace the pepper top and stand in an ovenproof dish. Add just enough stock to cover the base of the dish. Cover with foil and bake at 180° C (350° F / gas 4) for 25 to 30 minutes until tender, removing the foil for the last 5 minutes.

- Serve freshly cooked peppers with a tangy cheese sauce or a sweet tomato and herb sauce as an accompaniment to chicken, ham or fish.

- Place skinned pepper flesh in a blender with yoghurt and tomato or carrot juice. Whiz together and season with celery salt and black pepper. Pour over ice in a glass for a super speedy chilled smoothie or pour into a bowl to serve as a light summer soup.

- Chop up small pieces of fresh pepper and mix with finely chopped red onion, a little mango and a little red chilli (optional). Dress in olive oil and balsamic vinegar and serve as a tasty crunchy relish to top grilled tuna, swordfish or chicken.

- Pack slices of grilled and skinned peppers into a cling film-lined loaf tin with layers of sliced tomato, cucumber, grated carrot, spring onion and radish. Cover and press down for several hours. Drain off any juice – keep this for stocks and soups – and turn on to a serving plate. Serve as a colourful salad vegetable 'terrine' as part of a buffet.

# PLUMS, GREENGAGES AND DAMSONS

Plums can be grown in much the same way as pears and there are several self-fertilising varieties available. They need sun, warmth, shelter and good drainage, but flower very early so are not suitable for late-frost areas. Greengage trees are smaller and are even more susceptible to frosts. The damson is the hardiest variety and will thrive in the wettest areas where other plums will find it difficult; it is also self-fertile. Damsons make the bushiest tree however, so if space is short, you may find that the damson is not right for your patch, but they can be fan-trained to grow against a wall so this might be an option to look at. Choose compact varieties of plums and greengage if you are planning to train into a fan or cordon and growing in this way is by far the best method if space is restricted. If the tree is left to grow in its bush form, it will grow pretty large, so will be unsuitable for most allotments or small spaces. Plums can be yellow to rich red to purple in colour, with Victoria, a purplish-red plum, being a particular culinary favourite.

## HARVESTING, STORING AND PREPARATION

Harvest time for plums and greengages is August to September. Pick plums and greengages for cooking, preserving and freezing before they are quite ripe. For eating, leave them on the tree to ripen fully and they will be sweeter for it. If the weather is excessively wet, it is advisable to pick the fruit to avoid the skins splitting. Pull the fruit away from the tree with the stalk intact. Damsons should be ready to harvest in late August/September through to October. Pick by the stalks to avoid bruising.

As with most fruit, it is best used as soon after picking as possible. Sweet juicy plums are delicious eaten as a fresh fruit dessert, but there are varieties more suited to cooking. Wash plums and greengages, and wipe dry before eating. For cooking, cut along the indented part of the fruit and twist the halves apart; prise out the stone with the tip of a knife. Stew in a little water with some sugar to taste for about 10 minutes until soft. They can be halved and poached in a wine or sugar syrup by covering and cooking gently for 7 to 8 minutes. Damsons are usually cooked as they are less sweet. They are traditionally used in making jams and preserves, but do make a rich and fruity pie filling or compote. Prepare as for plums, but if the damsons are small you will have to use them whole and skim off the stones before serving – if you are unable to stone the fruit first, use 450 g (1 lb) damsons which will take about 15 minutes to cook down in 600 ml (1 pint) water. Once the stones are removed, thicken the cooking juices using an arrowroot paste. Otherwise, cook pitted damsons in just enough water to prevent them sticking for about 15 to 20 minutes for a good rich, compote. They will need quite a bit more sugar than plums and greengages.

## FREEZING

Avoid dry packing plums, greengages and damsons as the skin will be tough once thawed. Therefore, pack prepared in halves in rigid containers with a heavy sugar syrup with added lemon juice or in cooked or puréed form (see Peaches and Nectarines entry, pages 61–62).

## TOP TIPS FOR PLUMS, GREENGAGES AND DAMSONS

- Damsons are traditionally made into a 'cheese' to serve with rich meats. This is a thick puréed preserve made by cooking the sugar and damson mixture until very thick and sticky. Set in moulds or straight sided glass jars for easy unmoulding and slicing.
- Mix damsons with cooking apples to reduce the richness and to add bulk to fillings for pies and crumbles.
- A compote of damsons is ideally served with crushed brown sugar meringue and a dollop of clotted cream.
- Good flavours to go with plums include ginger, orange, star anise, bay leaves, red wine and cinnamon. And for greengages try vanilla or almond.
- Wrap whole large plums in marzipan and then buttered filo pastry and bake at 190° C (375° F / gas 5) for about 25 minutes to make crispy plum dumplings.
- Stew some sweet plums with red onion and fresh ginger. Allow to cool, then sweeten and add a shot of raspberry vinegar (see page 80) and serve hot or cold with duck.
- Toss slices of fresh sweet plums into salad leaves with some toasted walnuts and serve with smoked chicken and a vinaigrette dressing.
- Replace cooking apple with cooking plums in a traditional baked spiced red cabbage recipe.
- Replace apples with halves of greengage in a tarte Tatin recipe. Serve sprinkled with toasted flaked almonds and vanilla sugar.
- Bake prepared halves of plums in red wine, sprinkled with brown sugar and a little ground ginger for about 15 minutes at 200° C (400° F / gas 6). Simmer the juices down to make a syrup and serve the plums warm with mascarpone cheese or ginger ice cream.

# POTATOES

Simple to grow; very versatile; delicious to eat, and easy to prepare and cook, potatoes are very nutritious to boot. High in carbohydrate, low in fat, high in fibre and a good source of Vitamin C, this humble starchy vegetable is everyone's ultimate comfort food.

## VARIETIES AND SUITABILITY FOR COOKING

### 'NEW' OR 'EARLY' CROP

In season from May to August; cook as near to lifting as possible – the potatoes should be 'damp' to the touch and the skins will be easy to rub off. New potatoes are best served boiled, hot or cold. The texture is too close and firm for mashing, but they will 'crush' slightly (see tip page 75). Larger potatoes make well-flavoured chips and sautés.

**Common varieties include:** Home Guard, Maris Peer, Red Craigs Royal, Duke of York, Orla, Premiere and Cara.

### 'OLD' OR 'MAIN' CROP

In season from September to May. Discard spade-damaged, sprouting potatoes or those with green patched flesh – the green flesh has the potential to cause gastric upset. Different varieties are better suited for particular cooking purposes:

**Desirée** (red skinned), **Estima** and **Majestic** are good all-rounders but make excellent roasties, chips and sautés. These potato varieties have a firm or waxy flesh when cooked.

**King Edward, Pentland Hawk, Pentland White** and **Maris Piper** are also good for general use, but are especially good for boiling, mashes and baking in their skins. These potatoes have a floury texture when cooked.

**Charlotte, Belle de Fontenay** and **Pink Fir Apple** are smaller varieties which are perfect for boiling and serving hot or cold in salads.

## STORAGE

Potatoes are not hardy and should be lifted before the first frosts. They should be air dried before packing to prevent turning mouldy and discard any that are damaged or diseased. Pack in thick brown paper potato sacks, in a cool, frost-free dark, dry place for up to 3 months, and tie the top closed. These bags allow air to circulate and prevent light getting in – exposure to light will cause the potatoes to turn green. Small new potato varieties don't store very well, so use them up whilst they are in season. However, my grandfather used to bury a selection of new potatoes, still in their loose soil, in a biscuit tin in his garden and leave them undisturbed, until Christmas time. Six months later, Mum and the family would enjoy the flavour of freshly dug new potatoes with their Christmas turkey!

## PREPARATION AND BASIC COOKING TECHNIQUES

In general, wash (scrub if necessary using a small brush) and remove any 'eyes' or blemishes. Cook in their skins or thinly peel using a vegetable peeler or a small sharp knife, and cut according to cooking method. Remember that the greatest amount of nutrients lie just under the skin, so cut away as little as possible. Potatoes discolour if peeled and exposed to the air, so try and prepare them close to cooking. If you do want to prepare them in advance, cover them with cold water to keep the air out, but they will lose vitamin C.

• **Boiling**   Prepare as described above. Leave small ones whole and cut larger ones into even-sized pieces. Place in a saucepan and barely cover with cold water. Add a pinch of salt and bring to the boil. Cook, uncovered, for 12 to 15 minutes depending on their size, until just tender. Drain well and serve with melted butter and chopped parsley.

• **Steaming**   Small whole potatoes will take about 15 minutes to cook, whilst older potatoes, cut into pieces, may take up to 30 minutes.

• **Mash**   Prepare and cook old potatoes as for boiling. Drain and return to the saucepan. Mash using a fork or potato masher for a textured mash, or push through a ricer or beat with an electric mixer, for a smoother texture. Add butter, milk or cream to taste, then season and beat using a wooden spoon.

• **Chips**   Peel large potatoes thinly and cut into even-sized chips. Rinse well, drain off the water and dry thoroughly using kitchen paper. Preheat oil for deep frying to 150° C (300° F) and fry in small batches for about 4 minutes until tender but not browned. Drain very well on kitchen paper and allow to cool. Just before serving, heat the oil to 180° C (350° F) and fry the chips in batches for 2 to 3 minutes until golden brown. Drain well and serve immediately, dusted with salt or spices.

• **Roasties**   Peel the potatoes thinly and cut into even-sized pieces (you can leave smaller ones whole). Place in a saucepan and barely cover with cold water. Add a pinch of salt and bring to the boil. Cook, uncovered, for about 5 minutes. Drain well and allow to air dry for about 10 minutes. Return to the saucepan, cover, then shake the pan to 'rough up' the edges of the potatoes. Preheat the oven to 200° C (400° F / gas 6). Heat about 100 g (3½ oz) lard, dripping or goose fat or 6 tablespoons of sunflower oil in a shallow sided roasting tin for 5 minutes until very hot and carefully add the potatoes, tossing them in the hot fat to coat. Bake in the oven for about 40 to 50 minutes, turning occasionally, until golden and crisp all over. Drain and serve immediately.

• **Baked (in their jackets)**   Choose even-sized potatoes, scrub them clean, pat dry and prick them all over with a fork, to prevent them bursting during cooking. Preheat the oven to 200° C (400° F / gas 6). Place on a baking tray and brush all over with sunflower or olive oil, and sprinkle with salt and pepper. Bake for about 1 to 1½ hours depending on size, until tender – the potatoes will yield to gentle pressure when cooked sufficiently. To serve, make a slit in the top, then squeeze the potato gently through kitchen paper to open it slightly. Add a knob of butter or soft cheese and season with black pepper.

# FREEZING

• **New potatoes** Wash and scrape small, even-sized new potatoes. Cook in boiling, salted water until just tender. Drain well and toss in melted butter. Turn into a freezer bag and allow to cool. Seal, label and store for up to 6 months. To use, place the potatoes and butter in an ovenproof dish, cover and reheat in a preheated oven at 180° C (350° F / gas 4), for 30 to 40 minutes, stirring occasionally, until hot. Serve sprinkled with freshly chopped herbs.

• **Chips** Blanch uncooked chips in boiling water for 1 minute, drain and cool quickly. Open freeze until solid, then pack into freezer bags. Seal, label and store for up to 6 months. To use, defrost and cook in hot oil as above.

• **Mash** Prepare as described, and cool quickly. Pack in small portions in freezer containers or bags. Seal, label and freeze for up to 6 months. To use, allow to thaw, then place in a covered saucepan over a low heat with a little milk or cream and a knob of butter, and cook very gently, stirring occasionally, for about 10 minutes, until hot.

• **Roast** Cook as described, then drain and cool quickly. Pack into freezer bags, seal and label, and store for up to 6 months. To use, heat a little oil in a roasting tin and turn the frozen potatoes into it. Reheat at 190° C (375° F / gas 5) for about 30 minutes, turning occasionally, until hot.

• **Baked** Cook as described and cool quickly. Wrap in freezer foil, label and store for up to 6 months. To use, place still wrapped in a preheated oven at 200° C (400° F / gas 6) for about 35 minutes. Remove the foil and cook for a further 10 minutes to crisp up.

# TOP RECIPE TIPS FOR POTATOES

- For a healthier 'mash', lightly crush floury potatoes and stir in half fat crème fraîche or Greek yoghurt, lemon zest, plenty of chopped parsley and chives, and season well.

- For a comforting soup with a hint of tang, pop some prepared cooking apple slices into the potato water just before the end of cooking. Drain lightly and purée together. Season well and stir in butter, hot chicken stock and cream to taste.

- Roast scrubbed whole baby new potatoes and whole garlic cloves in olive oil with coarse salt and fresh herbs scattered on top – no par-boiling required.

- Toss diced or sliced cooked potato into egg as it scrambles or cooks in an omelette and serve with fried onion and black pepper for a light meal.

- Boil freshly scrubbed new potatoes in lightly salted water with a large sprig of fresh mint. Drain and 'crush' gently using a potato masher. Serve with a large dollop of mint and lemon butter to run over (or for a healthier option, add chopped mint and lemon zest to seasoned natural fromage frais).

- Liven up plain boiled potatoes or mash by making your own herb or spice butters. Simply spoon a dollop on to the potatoes just before serving.

- Dress whole baked potatoes by slicing 4 deep cuts in each and fill alternately with 2 slices of mozzarella cheese, sun-dried tomato in oil and some fresh pesto sauce. Return to the oven for a few minutes until the cheese melts.

- For healthy chips, prepare as described and place in a large bag with 2 tablespoons of sunflower oil. Seal and shake, then arrange evenly on a large baking sheet lined with baking parchment. Sprinkle with salt and spices, and bake in a preheated oven at 220° C (425° F / gas 7) for about 30 minutes, turning halfway through cooking, until tender and golden.

- Try replacing the grated carrot in a carrot cake recipe with cold, unseasoned smoothly-mashed potato, to give extra moistness.

- Halve freshly cooked baked potatoes and scoop out the hot potato flesh. Mash this with a dollop of soft cheese with garlic and herbs, some grated Cheddar cheese and a little beaten egg and pile back into the potato skins. Return to the oven and bake for a further 10 to 15 minutes until golden.

# PUMPKIN AND WINTER SQUASH

Closely related to the vegetable marrow, pumpkin and squash develop a hard skin when left to mature. They can be grown as a bush or trailing plant, but do take up quite a bit of space, and some varieties of pumpkin can reach huge proportions, so chose varieties carefully! Winter squashes come in all shapes and sizes and will certainly be the talking point of any patch, but the plants do tend to sprawl so are not really suitable if space is an issue.

## VARIETIES

**Pumpkin – Atlantic Giant** The name speaks for itself! You'll need space for this one. The smaller, orange and round **Triple Treat** has tasty flesh, and makes a good jack-o-lantern for Halloween.

**Winter squash – Butterball** Grows quickly and has sweet, soft-cooking, buttery orange flesh.

**Turks Turban** Has a skin multicoloured with splashes of orange, green and cream and is turban-shaped. It is grown for its eye-catching appeal, and in comparison, the very ordinary looking **Crown Prince** with greyish skin, has flesh that is nutty, sweet and delicious.

## HARVESTING, STORING AND PREPARATION

Allow to ripen on the ground until they sound hollow when tapped. Harvesting time is usually between September and October depending on the variety. For storing over winter, it is a good idea to turn over the fruit and dry the underside in the sun before lifting and storing in a dry, frost-free shed for later use.

Traditionally pumpkin flesh is made into a purée and used as a mash, soup or sweet pie filling, but as with squash, it does make a colourful and earthy vegetable accompaniment. Depending on the size of the beast you'll probably need quite a heavy duty knife or cleaver to cut the pumpkin or squash in half. Scrape out the seeds and stringy membranes and cut into chunks for slow roasting around a meat joint with the skin on – this will take about 1 hour. Alternatively, slice off the skin and cut into small chunks. Cook in lightly salted water for 15 to 20 minutes before draining well and serving as a vegetable, or mashing with butter and a little nutmeg. You can also roast chunks of pumpkin and squash without the skin, seasoned and sprinkled with olive oil and a little butter, for about 40 to 50 minutes at 200° C (400° F / gas 6) basting occasionally until tender and slightly charred.

## FREEZING

Not recommended for freezing as they tend to be too soft and watery on thawing. If you do want to freeze some, it is best made into a purée for using as a pie filling or soup base. Store for up to 12 months, then thaw and drain before using.

## TOP RECIPE TIPS FOR PUMPKIN AND SQUASH

- Good flavours for seasoning include cinnamon, nutmeg, black pepper, mild curry powder, celery salt, orange, chilli and ginger.
- The seeds of some varieties of pumpkin (Triple Treat) are excellent toasted and served as a snack.
- Drizzle chunks of pumpkin or squash with maple syrup or sprinkle with brown sugar before baking in orange juice and butter, for a savoury/sweet vegetable accompaniment to roast chicken and cranberry sauce.
- Boiled pumpkin or squash can be served as an accompanying vegetable with a blue cheese or chilli tomato sauce poured over. Good with pork dishes.
- Replace grated carrot with pumpkin or squash purée in a carrot cake recipe for moistness and golden colour.
- Blend pumpkin or squash purée with chicken stock, onion, garlic and a little cream to make a hearty autumnal soup. Serve with cheesy bread.
- Fold cold pumpkin or squash purée into pancake batter or beaten eggs for omelettes to add texture, flavour and colour. Season with nutmeg and a few chopped chives.
- Pumpkin leaves can be eaten if small and fresh. Peel the spiky back stem away using a vegetable peeler, wash and cut up like large spinach leaves. Simmer in oil with chopped tomato, salt and a little cream. They should be tender in about 10 minutes.
- Spread rounds of puff pastry with seasoned thick pumpkin or squash purée and top with rounds of goat's cheese or crumbled blue cheese and bake until crisp.
- Hollow out small pumpkins and squash, and use the flesh for soup or toss into pasta or risotto. Bake the shells until tender and use as a serving bowl for the main dish.

# RADISH

The Ancient Egyptians grew radish and the vegetable was probably introduced to Britain by the Romans. You can grow winter and summer varieties for cooking and salad use respectively. Summer radishes are amongst the quickest growing of vegetables and can be grown all year round if protected from frosts by cloches; the root can be rounded or elongated, pink, red, white or purple. Winter radish, which include the Oriental mooli or daikon, can grow longer than a parsnip and the leaves can be eaten like cabbage; the flesh is white but the skin can be white, red, green, yellow, purple and black, and the flavour can be mildly peppery to very spicy and hot.

## HARVESTING, STORING AND PREPARATION

From 4 to 6 weeks after sowing, summer radishes are ready for pulling. Pull as many as are needed when they are young and tender. Winter radish roots can be left in the ground until required, but they will store in boxes of sand in a cool, airy place over the winter. Both varieties can be used raw in salads, with cheese or as a crudité or garnish. Trim away the root and top for salads, but leave a 2.5 cm (1 in) shoot of stalk if serving as a dipper or cheese board accompaniment. Wash and pat dry before serving. For cooking larger radish, scrub or even peel if the skin is blemished or tough. Cook whole or diced if very large in lightly salted boiling water for 7 to 10 minutes until tender. Drain and season with black pepper and butter. Black radish can be pungent and is often salted before being used like celery in a salad.

## FREEZING

Not suitable.

## TOP RECIPE TIPS FOR RADISH

- Fresh radish makes a delicious sandwich filling – try slicing and seasoning with salt and pepper and serving on buttered brown or rye bread. Also good with egg mayonnaise.
- For a traditional radish garnish, choose round radish, trim off the root and make 6 to 8 small cuts down and around the radish from root to stalk end, taking care not to sever the slices. Leave in iced water to open out like flower petals. Longer radishes can be cut through down their length to just below the stalk in thin strips. Leave in iced water to open out. These flowers look great served as a decoration for hors d'oeuvre.
- Add radish leaves to spinach whilst cooking, or blend into a purée and add to mashed potato.
- Serve lightly cooked radish with a well seasoned parsley sauce as a side dish for fish or chicken.

# RASPBERRY AND LOGANBERRY (including tayberry, boysenberry, veitchberry and youngberry)

Among the most well loved and tasty of all summer fruits, raspberries grow well throughout the cooler parts of the northern hemisphere. Full sun will produce the best crop, but partial shaded sites are also suitable. Raspberries give a good yield and they freeze well, so can be enjoyed all year round. Different varieties fruit at different times: summer-fruiting from July and August, and autumn fruiting from September to October. Much easier to tame than blackberries, various hybrids have been developed by crossing the two fruits, and these require the same growing conditions as raspberries. The loganberry is one of the most successful and delicious of the hybrids, with larger, longer fruits and a sharper more acidic flavour. Other hybrids include the tayberry, boysenberry, youngberry and veitchberry; the flavour varies according to their origin but they can be used in exactly the same ways as raspberries or blackberries.

## HARVESTING, STORING AND PREPARATION

Pick raspberries when they are evenly and richly coloured. They should come away easily, leaving the white core behind on the stalk. Once picked they won't keep well, so eat or freeze as soon after harvesting as possible, storing them unwashed in the refrigerator until required. Loganberries ripen in August, midway between raspberries and blackberries. Pick when dry, deep dark red, acid and juicy. Use them quickly whether eating fresh, preserving or cooking. Remember that the birds like your berries just as much as you do, so keep them covered with netting!

As with all berries, these fruits bruise easily so handle with care. Place in single layers in a colander and dip in cold water to rinse. Drain well and pat dry with kitchen paper before serving. Eat fresh with a squeeze of lemon juice, crunchy white sugar and thick cream. For many desserts, raspberries are made into a purée in order to remove the seeds. Push the berries through a nylon sieve using a wooden spoon, into a bowl, or whiz in a blender or food processor first. Sweeten with icing sugar, maple syrup, sugar syrup or honey. If serving hot, raspberries and loganberries require only minimal poaching in a little liquid and sugar before they go mushy – 2 to 3 minutes is all it takes to heat them through for a compote. Like blackberries they do mix well with apples and pears for a pie filling. Perfect for mousses and creamy desserts, ice creams and sorbets, jams, jellies and other preserves.

## FREEZING

See Blackberries entry (pages 27–28).

## TOP RECIPE TIPS FOR RASPBERRIES, ETC.

- **To make your own raspberry vinegar:** place 250 g (9 oz) prepared berries in a non reactive bowl and pour over 600 ml (1 pint) white wine vinegar. Cover and leave for 24 hours in a cool place. The next day, strain the liquid and discard the fruit. Place another 250 g (9 oz) fruit in a non reactive bowl and pour over the fruited vinegar. Cover and leave as before. The next day, strain the liquid through muslin and discard the fruit. Put another 150 g (5½ oz) berries in a large sterilised bottle or jar and pour over the fruited vinegar. Seal well and leave to stand in a cool, dark place for at least 1 month before using. Can also be used for blackberries.

- Vanilla-, rose- or lavender-scented sugar, or a light sprinkling of rose water or orange flower essence enhance the perfumed flavour of fresh raspberries.

- Toss fresh berries into a salad with cubed sweet melon and dress with raspberry vinegar (see above) and honey dressing. Serve with thick-sliced ham.

- Serve fresh berries with a homemade fresh orange juice jelly.

- Serve a chocolate mousse or cheesecake with a fresh raspberry purée or coulis for extra zing.

- Sprinkle berries into the base of ramekins before topping with a crème brûlée custard.

- Lightly crush fresh raspberries with a little sugar and use as a fresh spread to dollop on top of clotted cream on scones or lightly toasted brioche.

- Place a few raspberries in the bottom of a fluted wine glass. Spoon over sweetened raspberry purée or crème de cassis and top with chilled sparkling wine or champagne.

- Sprinkle fresh berries over your morning bowl of breakfast cereal instead of sugar for a healthier alternative.

- Whiz fresh berries in a blender with apple or orange juice. Sieve if preferred and use as super-fruity base for making your own ice lollies.

# RHUBARB

Grows best in an open site but will grow anywhere, although rhubarb does like a good mulching, remembering that the roots of an established plant run deep. It is easy to cultivate and a single plant will provide a good yield for a small family. The rhubarb stalks are the only edible part of the plant – the leaves are poisonous. Once rhubarb has established – after 3 years – plants can be forced for early cropping. This rhubarb will be thinner stalked, softer and pinker than those stalks left to mature unforced.

## HARVESTING, STORING AND PREPARATION

Don't pick any stems in the first year. In the second year, pull a few stems, leaving about half on the plant, and stop around mid summer to allow the plant to recover. In the following years, pull fully grown stems as needed. To pull, place your thumb inside the stem as far down as you can, and twist to pull it away from the crown. Do not cut the stems. Cut off and discard the leaves.

Rhubarb is very acidic and requires a lot of sweetening to make it palatable. But its clean taste makes it an excellent choice of dessert to follow a rich, creamy main course. Prepare young, forced rhubarb stalks by trimming off the leafy tops and the pale pink root. Wash and dry thoroughly. Older rhubarb can develop a coarse stringy skin which should be peeled. Trim and wash as before. Cut rhubarb into desired lengths and either poach in syrup for about 10 minutes until tender or bake uncooked in a pie, crumble or tart. Rhubarb goes well with redcurrants and raspberries, and makes good jams and preserves.

## FREEZING

Choose tender young stalks and prepare as above. Cut into 2.5 cm (1 in) lengths and dry pack in rigid containers or freezer bags. Blanching is unnecessary. Keep for up to 6 months. Use for stewed fruit and pies. Alternatively pack as above but pour over a heavy sugar syrup – see Peaches and Nectarines entry (pages 61–62), omitting the lemon juice. Use in pies, fools and crumbles. Can also be stewed or puréed and frozen.

## TOP RECIPE TIPS FOR RHUBARB

- Flavours to temper rhubarb's acidity are ginger, cinnamon, orange, angelica and liquorice.
- Make a tangy stewed rhubarb sauce – add a dash of raspberry vinegar (see page 80) and brown sugar – to serve with smoked or grilled mackerel.
- Stew and cool sweetened rhubarb, then whiz in a blender with ripe banana. Layer in a glass with whipped cream or yoghurt and crumbled shortbread biscuits.

# SALAD LEAVES

If you decide to grow salad leaves on your plot you'll be spoilt for choice and they don't need a special bed; you can put them between slow-to-mature vegetables like parsnips as the leaves will be picked long before the other crop needs more space. Salad leaves are not suitable for freezing.

## LOOSE LEAF LETTUCE

These lettuces have little or no solid hearts and will be ready to harvest between 4 and 14 weeks after planting depending on variety:

**Salad bowl** A bright green or bronze-edged frilly soft-leaved large lettuce with a mild, earthy flavour. Leaves are usually picked as required.

**Oak leaf or feuille de chêne** Shaped like the leaves of the oak tree, the leaves are soft and green and reddish-tinted with a slightly bitter flavour.

**Lollo biondo and lollo rosso** A bright green and a red variety of frilly soft-leaved lettuce with a delicate flavour.

### HARVESTING AND PREPARATION

Either cut with a sharp knife just above ground level, or pull out completely and trim away the root afterwards. Cut away the root end and discard any damaged outer leaves. Wash lightly in cold water and dry thoroughly in a salad spinner or kitchen paper. Avoid washing the tender inner hearts as these easily become water-logged. Small leaves can be left whole, but larger leaves are best shredded by tearing rather than cutting with a knife.

## COS LETTUCE

Crisp leaved right to the centre, ready to harvest between 4 and 14 weeks after planting, depending on variety:

**Little Gem** Small, firmly packed and delicious with pale green sweet leaves in the centre.

**Lobjoit's Green Cos** A well known classic cos lettuce with long crisp leaves. Central leaves are perfect for dipping.

### HARVESTING AND PREPARATION

As above.

## CRISPHEADS AND BUTTERHEADS

These lettuces have a firm heart and will be ready to harvest between 4 and 14 weeks after planting, depending on variety. **Webb's Wonderful** is probably the best known and much loved of these types of lettuce.

### HARVESTING AND PREPARATION

As above.

## ENDIVE AND BATAVIA OR ESCAROLE

The leaves are related to chicory and dandelion and have the same 'bitter' flavour. When combined with other leaves they make an interesting addition to a salad bowl. Ready to harvest around 12 weeks after planting:

**Frisée** Very frilly fine bright green to yellowy leaves, makes a great garnish and a good 'nesty' base for a salad bowl. It is rich in folic acid.

**Batavia or escarole** Broad crisper green leaves with a slightly bitter flavour.

### HARVESTING AND PREPARATION

As above.

## CHICORY (INCLUDING WITLOOF, RADICCHIO AND SUGARLOAF

Grows in the same conditions as other lettuces and adds another dimension to the salad bowl with its crisp texture, splash of colour and bitter flavour. Can be grown as cut-and-come again crops:

**Witloof or Belgian chicory** White leaved, ready for eating in winter.

**Radicchio or red chicory** Rounded, tightly packed small purplish pink leaved chicory with bright white veining, for autumn eating. **Treviso** is more chicory shaped.

**Sugarloaf** Large hearted green Cos-like chicory. The outer leaves are discarded and the pale centre is pleasantly mild tasting. Ready for autumn eating.

### HARVESTING AND PREPARATION

Ready for picking when the chicons are about 15 cm (6 in) high or after about 4 weeks of forcing (chicory plants are sown in May/June, lifted in October/November, and then potted and covered in order to force the chicons to develop). Cut just before using, as above. Remove the root end and the outer leaves. Halve and discard any core that has formed. Use fresh, or boil or steam for 10 to 15 minutes. Drain well and serve with butter, bechamel or hollandaise sauce.

## CORN SALAD (LAMB'S LETTUCE OR MACHE)

A gourmet salad leaf rich in Omega 3 with tender soft green leaves and a delicate fresh lettucy flavour. It grows easily and self-seeds if permitted. If covered it will survive throughout the winter months so is excellent value. French varieties are like tiny compact lettuces and can be lifted whole and used as a garnish. English and Dutch varieties are more spreading.

### HARVESTING AND PREPARATION

Ready for use after the fourth pair of leaves form. Either use the whole plant and simply snip off at the roots, or pick a few larger leaves. They wilt quickly so use as soon as possible. The leaves grow close to the ground so get quite earthy, and need careful rinsing and drying before use.

## ROCKET

A salad brassica often classed as a herb but frequently used in the salad bowl, the small dark green slightly feathery leaves have a spicy, peppery flavour. Easy to grow although the leaves seed quickly and need frequent watering. Can be grown as a cut-and-come again crop. Leaves will be ready to harvest from 4 to 12 weeks after sowing.

### HARVESTING AND PREPARATION

Pick individual young leaves or cut off the tops completely. The leaves will re-sprout several times. Older leaves will have a stronger flavour and coarser texture. Rinse and carefully pat dry.

## TOP RECIPE TIPS FOR SALAD LEAVES

- Halve radicchio or Little Gem lettuce and place on the BBQ for about 30 seconds on each side to just wilt. Serve this smoky salad vegetable warm with a garlic or chilli dressing.
- Finely shred a well flavoured lettuce and cook lightly with shredded leek in chicken or vegetable stock until just tender. Blend until smooth. Season with nutmeg and stir in cream to serve as a delicate flavoured soup.
- Lightly blanch thick lettuce leaves. Cool in iced water, pat dry and use for crisp wrappings for Chinese vegetables and sticky rice. Serve with a tasty dipping sauce.
- Braise lettuce hearts in a little stock with bacon and onion for serving as a side dish with fish.
- Pile mounds of fresh rocket leaves on top of pizzas, risottos and pasta for a stylish garnish.
- Serve chicory leaves with orange, ugli or pink grapefruit segments and a honey dressing.

# SPINACH AND CHARD

A favourite with Popeye, spinach has made a comeback in recent years, mostly as a salad leaf, because of its excellent nutritional content. Spinach likes a cool climate, fertile soil and damp surroundings. You'll need to sow several plants to get a good yield. It can be sowed as a cut-and-come-again crop, or allowed to mature. There are differing varieties that will provide a crop all year round. Stunning red veined varieties of chard are also a popular addition to the modern-day salad bowl and the leaves have a mild beetroot taste.

**Summer spinach** Sown in March to July and ready for harvesting in June to October. This is the broad, rounded leaf variety that we are most familiar with. Young leaves can be picked and tossed into salads, whilst mature leaves are better cooked.

**New Zealand spinach** Grows on bushy stems, and the leaves are more pointed; it takes up more space than other spinach. This variety is better for dry conditions where the soil is poor, but it is not hardy and will be killed by frost. Ready for harvesting from June to September, it can be used the same as Summer spinach, but the midribs of the mature leaves are not eaten.

**Spinach beet or perpetual spinach** Produces a succession of leaves over a long period and is probably the easiest to grow. The flavour can be more peppery than other spinach types, but can be used in the same way. It doesn't keep long after picking, so must be used fresh.

**Chard (Swiss chard, ruby chard, seakale beet, silver chard, silver beet)** The succulent leaves and stalks of a variety of beet, there are so many to choose from, you can make a multicoloured display of leaves if you grow several different types of leaves. The bright colours do disappear on cooking, but like other spinach, small young leaves make tasty salad or garnish. For cooking, the larger green-leaved chard with its stunning white stems is regarded as the tastiest – the leaves and stems are usually cooked separately, the stems treated like asparagus – but on the whole the flavour is less pronounced than spinach and the nutritional content is not so high. By sowing chards in different stages, you should be able to grow an all year round supply.

## HARVESTING, STORING AND PREPARATION

With all types of spinach, pick the leaves when they are ready. Even when not wanted for the kitchen, it is best to pick the leaves of spinach beet, New Zealand spinach and seakale beet regularly to encourage more growth. Pick a few outside leaves before they become tough, but avoid taking more than 50 per cent of the plant otherwise it will be unable to regenerate.

All spinach wilts quickly after picking, so pick to order and use straight away whilst still crisp. Young leaves for eating raw just need immersing in cold water to remove any soil, and then rinsed and dried in the same way as lettuce. For cooking, mature leaves are best stripped from the stalks and coarse midribs and then broken up or left whole. Immerse in cold water, several times, until the water is clear of soil and grit. Shake off the excess water but don't dry. Pack the wet spinach leaves into a saucepan and add a pinch of salt. You don't need to add any more water for cooking – the leaves will cook in the steam. Cover with a tight fitting lid and cook over a gentle heat for 5 to 6 minutes until wilted. Drain in a colander, pressing out as much of the water as possible – a potato masher is a good tool to use here. Traditionally served with nutmeg and butter.

For large varieties of chard leaves like Swiss, remove the green parts of the leaves, and break off (not cut) the stalks and veins; remove the stringy parts. Break the stalks into sections about 5 cm (2 in) long, and rip the leaves into small pieces. Cook the leaves like spinach and the stalks like asparagus. Traditionally chicken or vegetable stock is used instead of plain water because the vegetable is usually served with the cooking liquid made into a white sauce to add more flavour.

## FREEZING

Choose young spinach and prepare as above. Blanch in small quantities for 2 minutes. Drain well and press out excess water. Allow to cool. Pack into rigid containers or freezer bags. Seal and store for up to 12 months. Cook from frozen with a small amount of water. Cover and cook for about 5 minutes, stirring occasionally to break up. Drain well and serve with butter.

## TOP TIPS FOR SPINACH AND CHARD

- In order for the body to absorb as much of spinach's rich iron content, always serve the vegetable with a good source of vitamin C such as a glass of freshly squeezed orange juice, or make a spinach and orange salad, or chop some fresh tomato and sprinkle on top.
- Spinach is popular in the Middle East and is delicious stirred into a chickpea and tomato stew. Stir leaves into the nearly cooked mixture and flavour with cumin, cinnamon and coriander.
- For a low calorie Florentine mixture, cook wet spinach leaves with shredded leek as described above, and replace cream and butter with fromage frais. Serve as a bed for steamed smoked haddock and top with fresh chopped tomato.
- Swiss chard torte is a speciality of Nice and is served as a dessert. Chopped leaves are mixed with cooking apples, lemon, dried fruit, almonds and pine nuts, sweetened and baked in a pastry case. It is served hot or cold dredged in icing sugar.
- Sauté mixed mushrooms with shallots and garlic and toss in spinach leaves. Stir-fry for a couple of minutes and add a little cream and blue cheese to make a sauce. Sprinkle with thyme and serve on toasted crusty bread as a light supper or filling for a warm pastry case.

# STRAWBERRIES

Without doubt most people's favourite soft fruit, which is rewarding and easy to grow. There are many different varieties which offer crops of berries from the end of May right through to October. Strawberry plants grow forming good ground cover and can be used to make an informal edging on a plot, particularly alpine varieties. They like well drained, moisture retentive soil that's well fed, and sunshine and water will help give a good crop. Mid season strawberries will give a good crop in the first year, whilst early and late varieties need to be held back to crop in the second year. Runners should be removed to conserve the plant's energy, but if you want to pot them up for use next year, keep no more than four on each plant.

## VARIETIES

**Honeoye**  Early crop with firm, glossy fruits.

**Pegasus**  Mid-season, big juicy fruits.

**Cambridge Favourite**  Mid-season, medium-sized juicy bright fruits.

**Hapil**  Mid-season, good yield with excellent flavour.

**Aromel**  Late season, large fruits.

**Alpine**  Much smaller fruits with a sweet perfumed flavour. Fruits ripen from June to October, and although time consuming to pick, they are much prized by culinary experts. The plants need not take up space in the fruit beds but can be grown in borders. They are prolific spreaders and will soon reproduce and provide many more plants.

## HARVESTING, STORING AND PREPARATION

Pick strawberries by the stalk to avoid bruising and eat as soon as possible after picking. Unless using as a decoration or dipper, remove the green calyx and stalk by carefully pulling it out (hulling). Rinse in a colander in cold water, drain and pat dry.

Leave alpine strawberries to ripen fully as they will have the most flavour. Pick regularly to encourage more fruits to form. Once picked the fruit doesn't keep longer than a day in the fridge. I freeze mine whole for use in jam because there never seems to be enough to serve fresh at the same time. If you do have sufficient, mix into a bowl of larger berries and serve with thick cream and sugar. Wash and pat dry as above. Strawberries are best eaten fresh as they tend to go soft and flabby if cooked, but if you do want them hot, poach in a little sugar syrup for 4 to 5 minutes and serve warm spooned over ice cream. Strawberries make excellent jams, preserves and syrups, and perfectly combine with cream in ices, mousses and custards. Strawberries can also be dried (see page 187).

## FREEZING

As for raspberries, but strawberries do go very soft after defrosting so they are best used in sauces, mousses and creams.

## TOP RECIPE TIPS FOR STRAWBERRIES

- For really sweet strawberries, halve and sprinkle with balsamic vinegar and black pepper, and serve with fresh cheese as a starter or an alternative to after-dinner cheeses.
- Whiz prepared strawberries to make a purée and mix with yoghurt, then freeze in moulds to make healthy ice lollies.
- Make them go further by placing in a dish and sprinkling with sugar and a little dessert wine or Pernod. Cover and chill for a few hours until the sugar melts. Serve at the base of serving dishes topped with good quality vanilla ice cream.
- Blend strawberries with other berries to make a purée. Sweeten with strawberry jam and use as an instant fruity sauce for ice cream. This can be frozen.
- Try flavouring a strawberry sorbet mixture with tarragon or lavender or add a little passion fruit juice to heighten the scented flavour of the fruit.
- If you have sufficient alpine strawberries, whip cream with dessert wine and spoon in a dish, swirling with strawberry jam and sprinkling the strawberries as you go. Chill for 2 hours before serving on top of meringues.
- For a grown-up fruit salad, serve alpine and halved strawberries in a combination of sweetened lime juice, dry white wine and crème de cassis. Chill together and serve sprinkled with freshly chopped mint.
- Strawberries mix well with smoked salmon or Parma ham and peppery leaves like rocket or watercress in a salad.
- Add rosewater or a few rose petals when making strawberry jam to increase the perfumed flavour.
- Mash strawberries lightly with a little vanilla sugar and fold into soft cheese. Spread over warm pancakes and serve with maple syrup.

# SWEDE, TURNIP AND KOHLRABI

I've put these three vegetables together because they are quite similar to use, but not to grow. Swede (or turnip in Scotland) is a field crop and does benefit from space and no shade. It is extremely hardy and provides a good vegetable source in winter months. The flavour is sweetly earthy and the texture firm. White turnips grow quickly and are picked young so are excellent if space is short. They may be grown between slower to mature roots and will be ready for picking long before crops such as parsnips are ready to develop. You should be able to plan crops for spring, summer and autumn, and white, yellow and red varieties are available. Turnip has a watery, peppery flavour and care should be taken not to overcook, as the flesh can easily become soggy. Kohlrabi is not a root but a swollen stem, and the flavour is somewhere between a turnip and a cabbage. It copes better with drier conditions than swede and turnip, and is ready for harvesting in autumn. Skin colour varies from green, white or purple. Unlike the leaves of swede and turnip, kohlrabi leaves are not eaten.

## HARVESTING, STORING AND PREPARATION

Swede roots can be lifted from autumn to winter as required, and some can be left in the ground for greens. For storing beyond this period, lift the roots and cut back the leaves to the top of the root. Keep in a cool, airy outbuilding ready for use when the soil is frozen. Prepare by cutting a thick slice off the top and bottom to reveal the yellowy flesh. Slice off the thick skin. Wash in cold water and cut into cubes or slices. Boil in lightly salted water for 15 to 20 minutes depending on size, until soft. Drain well and serve as is or mash with cream and butter. The sweet flavour is enhanced by adding a pinch of nutmeg or ginger to the mixture.

Pick turnips at about 6 weeks old and do it frequently so that they are not allowed to get very big – no larger than a tennis ball – otherwise the flavour will be impaired and the texture becomes stringy. Summer turnips can be frozen, whilst winter varieties can be pulled when needed, or stored as for swede. Prepare turnips by cutting off the leafy top and the root end. Peel young turnips thinly, and main crop turnips more thickly. Wash well. Young turnips can be left whole, whilst others are best cut up. Cook young turnips in a lightly salted water for about 15 to 20 minutes, and turnip pieces for about the same depending on size. Drain well. Young turnips are lovely glazed with sugar and butter, or served with parsley sauce. Other turnip can be mashed and seasoned with lemon juice and a little nutmeg or mace as a traditional accompaniment along with swede, to the Scottish classic dish, haggis.

For kohlrabi, pull the plants from the soil by the bulbous stem when it reaches the size of a golf or tennis ball, depending on variety. If left they will continue to grow and become tough.

If the weather is mild, you should be able to leave them in the ground until early winter. Eat shortly after harvesting. To prepare, cut off the leafy tops and trim away the root. Scrub thoroughly in running water. For eating raw, peel and grate coarsely for adding to salads, or peel and cut into fingers or small chunks ready for cooking. Cook in a small amount of lightly salted water for about 10 minutes. Drain well and serve as an accompanying vegetable with butter and black pepper or mash as above.

## FREEZING

Swede is not recommended for freezing as it goes very watery and loses texture. For turnips and kohlrabi, choose small roots, and trim and prepare as above. Blanch for 2 minutes, drain, cool and pack into rigid containers or freezer bags. Store for up to 12 months and cook from frozen for 8 to 10 minutes. Larger turnips can be cut into dice ready for adding to stews or for mashing. Blanch as for baby turnips and store in the same way. Cook as above.

## TOP TIPS FOR SWEDE, TURNIP AND KOHLRABI

- Add chunks of swede and turnip to stews, and purée to soups to add bulk without adding starch – good if you're on the GI diet.
- Turnips are much loved by the French and are cooked and hollowed out, then baked and stuffed with cheesy risotto or a rich chopped mushroom mixture to serve.
- Caramelise lightly cooked kohlrabi with brown sugar and butter and serve as a side dish to accompany pork or sausages.
- Add grated raw kohlrabi to a coleslaw mix instead of some or all of the cabbage.
- Cook thin slices of swede, turnip and kohlrabi with potato and carrot, layered up in a buttered dish. Season well and add a little stock. Cover tightly with foil and a lid and cook slowly in the oven until meltingly tender, about 2 hours depending on depth, at 180° C (350° F / gas 4). Serve in scoops with a casserole or hearty stew.

# SWEET CORN

Developed from the maize crop which is grown extensively in America, sweet corn varieties have been developed to cope with the cooler British climate. As well as producing a fine crop of succulent sweet vegetables, the plant is easy to grow, and is tall with long draping leaves and fine feathery flowers which make an attractive display on the plot. The corn cobs can be yellow, creamy coloured, brown and even black, with varieties to plant throughout the year, even mini corns suitable for stir-frying. Apart from being popular with humans, birds and mice are also partial to the crop, so you will have to take relevant precautions.

## HARVESTING, STORING AND PREPARATION

Cobs are ready for picking about 6 weeks after the silvery silky tassels appear. The aim is to pick them before the sugar turns to starch to ensure they will be sweet and tender. The tassels will shrivel and turn brown as the seeds or kernels develop and change colour from light to deep. Carefully pull back the covering leaves from the cob and gently press a fingernail into one of the kernels; if it exudes a milky liquid the cobs should be picked and used, and if there is no liquid, the cob is well passed its prime. Either twist the cobs from the stalks or snap them off outwards. Use them quickly as they dry out quickly and lose their flavour. Strip off the outer leaves and silky strings. Cook whole in unsalted water for about 8 minutes – you can season lightly halfway through, but do not add at the beginning as this will toughen the kernels. You can also add a teaspoon of sugar to the water to develop the sweetness. Test for 'doneness' by pricking carefully with a skewer to see if the kernels are tender. Drain well and serve with black pepper and butter. You can either insert specially designed small forks at either end of the cob for easy picking up or use dessert forks. The kernels are simply bitten or gnawed off the cob to eat.

If you want to strip the cobs: before cooking, strip them off with a knife, and after cooking, you should be able to run a fork down the cob to remove them. Kernels bottle well to be enjoyed in winter months, and adding kernels to relishes and chutneys gives texture and 'bite'.

## FREEZING

Select young cobs and prepare as above. Blanch for about 4 minutes, cool and dry. Either wrap whole and pack into containers or freezer bags, or strip from the cobs as described above. Freeze for up to 12 months. Thaw whole cobs thoroughly before cooking for 6 to 7 minutes. Kernels can be cooked from frozen for about 5 minutes, or added directly to soups and casseroles.

# TOP RECIPE TIPS FOR SWEET CORN

- Sweet corn is even more delicious cooked over the barbecue. Strip away a few leaves keeping sufficient to cover the kernels, and remove the silky strings. Secure the remaining leaves with string, and then blanch whole for 4 minutes. Drain well. Cook over the barbecue, turning frequently, for about 5 to 6 minutes until tender.

- Stir kernels into a stiff pancake batter to make soft thick savoury drop scones – delicious flavoured with smoked paprika and chopped bacon. Alternatively fold kernels into a cheesy choux pastry mixture and deep fry to make fritters. Serve with sweet chilli sauce.

- Make a chowder by adding kernels to a thick, creamy potato and leek soup.

- For an Oriental flavours, simmer sweet corn cobs in coconut milk and serve sprinkled with chopped coriander and chilli.

- Creamed sweet corn is a lovely accompaniment to serve with roasted meats and grilled fish – simply cook the kernels and whiz in a blender with a little cream to make a purée. Reheat with a knob of butter and pinch of nutmeg.

# TOMATOES

Of all the fruits and vegetables you can grow yourself, the tomato has to be the one with the most marked difference in flavour compared to those commercially grown. The fresh smell of the vine and the juiciness and sweetness of the fruit is unique to home-grown tomatoes. Tomatoes come in all shapes, sizes and colours, from large beefy ones to tiny sweet cherry-like ones; they can be plum-shaped, pear-shaped, indented like pumpkins, and smooth and rounded. They come in various colours, including green, yellow, orange, red and purple, and even striped! Bush varieties are better for allotments as they can be grown outdoors and need no training; they are sprawling which makes them ideal for containers and tubs. Tomatoes need weekly feeding and watering to produce a good crop.

## VARIETIES FOR GROWING OUTDOORS

**Alicante**  Popular early tomato, with smooth red skin, very fine flavour.

**Golden sunrise**  Late season, small to medium-sized yellow fruit with a sweet flavour.

**Outdoor girl**  Ripens early with a good flavour.

**Tigerella**  A bush tomato with medium-sized fruit and striped skin.

**Tournado**  A bush tomato that produces lots of large red fruit with good flavour.

## HARVESTING, STORING AND PREPARATION

Outdoor tomatoes will be ready for picking from August through to October. Pick as they start to ripen. If tomatoes are left on the plants to ripen, the flavour is slightly better, but they will ripen successfully after picking. Hold the tomato in your hand and press the stalk with your fingers to break it neatly at the joint just above the fruit. Some recipes call for tomatoes still on the vine, so in these circumstances snip off a few tomatoes still attached to the stalk.

Place underripe tomatoes in a paper bag with a ripe banana or wrap individually in newspaper and leave indoors in the dark until ripe. Alternatively, a few tomatoes can be ripened on a sunny windowsill for a few days. Gather in the whole crop before the frosts start. Tomatoes will keep for a few days once ripe in the fridge, but as with most produce, they are best enjoyed as fresh as possible, and if they have been chilled, allow them to come back to room temperature before eating. Just before serving, rinse and pat dry and remove the calyx and stalk. Fresh tomatoes are delicious served simply with a sprinkling of salt and black pepper, or a dressing of balsamic vinegar and olive oil; fresh basil and crusty bread would complete the meal.

Cooked tomatoes make great soups, bases for casseroles, pasta dishes and sauces, and they can be grilled and baked. Green and red tomatoes are traditionally made into chutney and ketchups. They dry well (see page 176).

• **Grilled tomatoes** Cut in half, season and top with a small knob of butter. Grill under a medium/hot grill for 10 to 15 minutes until just softening and lightly browned. Serve with breakfast eggs, bacon and sausages, or as a side dish with smoked fish or chicken.

• **Baked or roasted** This can be done with individual tomatoes or small branches. Place in a baking dish and season. Drizzle with olive oil, top with a few sprigs of rosemary or thyme, or add a few bay leaves, and cook at 200° C (400° F / gas 6) for about 10 minutes until the skin bursts.

• **Skinning** Many recipes call for the skin to be removed. Place ripe tomatoes in a heatproof bowl, prick the stalk end with a fork and pour over boiling water. Leave for 1 minute and during this time the skin should start to split at the stalk end. Rinse in cold water to cool. Carefully peel off the skin.

• **Filleting** A slightly more wasteful way to prepare a tomato, but is often used for fine sauces or garnishes. Quarter a ripe tomato, and carefully scoop out the seeds – these can be used to flavour stocks for soups. Using a small sharp knife, carefully slice the tomato pieces between the skin and flesh, as though you were filleting a fish.

## FRESH TOMATO SAUCE

This is a classic Italian tomato sauce for using as the base for many recipes which makes approximately 600 ml (1 pint). Any herbs can be used in this recipe, or they can be omitted if preferred. Flavourings such as chopped onion, celery, carrot and garlic can also be added for extra flavour and texture.

• 1.25 kg (2 lb 12 oz) ripe plum or tasty tomatoes, rinsed and halved
• Large sprig each of rosemary, thyme and oregano
• 1 bay leaf
• 1 tsp caster sugar
• ½ tsp salt
• 50 g (2 oz) unsalted butter
• 2 Tbsp olive oil

Place the tomato halves in the bottom of a large saucepan or frying pan with a lid. Tie the herbs and bay leaf together and place on top of the tomatoes. Cover with a lid and cook over a low/medium heat for about 40 minutes until soft and collapsed – keep the heat quite low to prevent burning. Discard the herbs and push the tomatoes through a nylon sieve to form a thick juice, leaving a dry residue of skins and seeds in the sieve. Return to a clean saucepan and add the remaining ingredients. Heat gently until the butter melts, then simmer gently for about 35 minutes until thickened but still thin enough to pour. Use as per recipe or allow to cool, cover and store in the fridge until required for a maximum of 3 days. Freeze in ice cube trays for up to 6 months.

# TOP RECIPE TIPS FOR TOMATOES

- For slightly underripe or green tomatoes, cut in thick slices and dredge in cornmeal and grated Parmesan cheese. Fry in olive oil until golden and crisp on each side. Serve as a tasty light lunch on toasted bread.
- Bake tomatoes with a topping of fresh breadcrumbs, capers, chopped anchovies, slivers of garlic and a drizzle of olive oil. Great served with fish.
- Dress an assortment of sliced tomatoes with olive oil and sprinkle with lightly toasted cumin seeds, salt, black olives and freshly chopped coriander.
- For a fresh tomato salsa, fillet tomatoes and chop the flesh finely. Mix with chopped red pepper and a little red chilli. Season with vinegar, olive oil, a little sugar, salt and pepper. Serve as a topping for Mexican tortillas or tacos, or as a dip or garnish.
- Sweet tomato fillets can be added to a citrusy fruit salad with cubes of papaya as an unusual talking point. Dress with a sugar syrup and chill well before serving, sprinkled with mint.
- Slice fresh tomatoes thinly and place on a hot serving plate. Season and drizzle with olive oil, before topping with a cheesy mashed potato and grilled sausages or smoked fish.
- Make a savoury version of the classic summer pudding, by using a chopped up mixture of juicy tomatoes, onion and herbs as a filling for a basin lined with cheesy bread. Chill and serve with basil and garlic mayonnaise or pesto sauce.
- Flavour a tomato soup with orange juice and a little zest, for added zing.
- Make a classic gazpacho (Spanish tomato and raw vegetable soup) and add a dash of vodka and Tabasco sauce to make a Bloody Mary soup.
- For a quick tomato 'marmalade', sauté 2 chopped red onions and 1 clove crushed garlic in olive oil with 1 small red chilli until very soft. Add 225 g (8 oz) chopped tomatoes, 2 tablespoons of balsamic vinegar and 2 tablespoons of caster sugar. Season and cook gently until thick. Allow to cool, then store in the fridge for up to a week. Lovely served with cold meats and cheese.

# RECIPES

**Roast asparagus and new potato salad** *See page 129*

**Cream of Jerusalem artichoke soup** *See page 130*

**Grilled aubergine, red onion and raspberries** *See page 131*

**Fresh bean minestrone with rocket pesto**  *See page 132*

**Warm Turkish-style baby carrot salad**  *See page 133*

**Pea cakes and pea shoot salad**  *See page 137*

**Apple, blue cheese and celery risotto** *See page 139*

**Roast salmon with green bean salsa** *See page 141*

**Roast lamb and garlic with celeriac mash** *See page 143*

**Venison with blackberry sauce**  *See page 146*

**Stir-fried pork with broccoli and cucumber** *See page 147*

**Cauliflower biriyani with sweet carrot relish**  *See page 148*

**Stir-fried Brussels sprouts with pancetta** *See page 150*

**Sweet potato and spinach curry** *See page 152*

**Cheesy cauliflower and broccoli fritters** *See page 153*

**Ratatouille** *See page 157*

**French-style peas with lettuce and glazed radishes** *See page 159*

**Potato and Jerusalem artichoke focaccia** *See page 161*

**Cherry tomato and sweet pepper upside-down tart** *See page 163*

**Blushing apples with strawberry rose ice cream** *See page 164*

**Blueberry pie with lavender cream** *See page 166*

**Blackcurrant fool** *See page 167*

**Oaty Scottish berry cream**  *See page 168*

**Trio of sorbets**  *See page 169*

**Rhubarb and custard tarts** *See page 170*

**Raspberry and redcurrant cheesecake** *See page 172*

**Marinated artichoke hearts with herbs and garlic** *See page 174*

**Baby aubergines in spiced oil**  *See page 175*

**Redcurrant and mint jelly** *See page 179*

**Sweet piccalilli**  *See page 182*

**Blackcurrant cordial** *See page 184*

**Spiced pears** *See page 185*

# SOUPS, STARTERS, LIGHT MEALS AND SALADS

## Roast asparagus and new potato salad  *See Page 97*

I love asparagus and this, to my mind, is the best way to eat it: lightly roasted in a hot oven so that the tips go slightly crispy. You can use whatever salad leaves and herbs you have and the flowers are a pretty, but optional, addition.

**Serves 4**

- 450 g (1 lb) baby new potatoes, scrubbed and halved
- 3 Tbsp olive oil
- 2 tsp coarse salt
- Freshly ground black pepper
- 350 g (12½ oz) asparagus spears
- 12 quail's eggs
- 1 small ripe avocado
- 1 Tbsp freshly squeezed lime juice
- 4 Tbsp mayonnaise
- 4 sticks celery with leaves
- Celery salt, to season
- 2 handfuls of assorted salad leaves, rinsed
- Small bunch of soft-leaved fresh herbs such as parsley, dill, chives, basil, marjoram
- Few fresh herb flowers (optional)

1 Preheat the oven to 200° C (400° F / gas 6). Place the new potatoes in a bowl and toss in 2 tablespoons of olive oil. Place in a shallow roasting dish and sprinkle with salt and pepper. Bake for 30 to 35 minutes, turning occasionally, until golden and tender. Drain well and keep warm.

2 Trim about 2.5 cm (1 in) away from the woody ends of the asparagus and arrange flat on a small baking sheet. Brush with the remaining olive oil and bake in the oven for about 25 minutes, turning occasionally, until tender and lightly crisp. Drain well and keep warm.

3 Meanwhile, place the quail's eggs in a small saucepan of water. Bring to the boil and cook for 4 minutes. Plunge immediately into iced water and set aside. Halve and stone the avocado, and peel off the skin. In a bowl, roughly chop the flesh and toss in the lime juice. Place in a blender or food processor and add the mayonnaise along with the leaves from the celery. Blend for a few seconds until smooth. Season with celery salt, cover and chill until required.

4 When ready to serve, carefully peel the quail's eggs and thinly slice the celery stalks. Arrange a few salad leaves, some herbs and sliced celery on four serving plates. Top with warm asparagus and potatoes. Halve the eggs and place on top. Serve each portion with a dollop of avocado mayonnaise and sprinkle with herb flowers if liked. Serve immediately.

❄ **FREEZING**  Not suitable

# Cream of Jerusalem artichoke soup  *See Page 98*

A simple combination of ingredients to show off this under-used root vegetable at its best. You can also serve this soup cold. The 'crisps' make a lovely snack on their own.

**Serves 4**

**For the soup**

- 1 large lemon
- 1 kg (2 lb 3 oz) Jerusalem artichokes
- 25 g (1 oz) butter
- 1 large onion, peeled and finely chopped
- 900 ml (32 fl oz) chicken or vegetable stock
- 150 ml (5 fl oz) double cream
- Salt and white pepper

**For the crisps**

- Sunflower oil, for deep frying
- Freshly chopped parsley, to garnish

1 Cut the lemon in half and squeeze the juice into a large bowl. Half fill with cold water. Peel the artichokes, putting them in the lemony water as you go. Leave 150 g (5½ oz) whole and cut the remaining artichokes into small pieces, and place back in the lemony water.

2 Heat the butter in a large saucepan until bubbling and gently cook the onion for 5 to 6 minutes until softened but not browned, then remove the chopped artichokes with a slotted spoon and add to the pan along with the stock. Bring to the boil, then cover and simmer gently for 25 to 30 minutes until tender. Remove from the heat and cool for 10 minutes.

3 Transfer to a blender or food processor and blend for a few seconds until smooth. Return to the saucepan, stir in the cream and season to taste. When ready to serve, reheat until piping hot.

4 To make the artichoke crisps, heat the oil for deep frying to 190° C (375° F). Drain the reserved artichokes and slice very thinly. Pat dry using absorbent kitchen paper and then deep fry a few slices at a time for 4 to 5 minutes until crisp and golden. Drain on kitchen paper and keep warm whilst frying the other slices. Serve the soup, hot or cold, with a few crispy slices floating on the top. Garnish with a sprinkling of chopped parsley.

**COOK'S NOTE** The method for making the artichoke crisps would be the same for carrots, parsnips, beetroot or potatoes. Make sure you cut the vegetables as thinly as possible and dry them thoroughly before frying.

**FREEZING** Make the soup as above but omit the cream. Allow to cool, then pack into freezer soup bags or a freezer-proof container. Seal, label and freeze for up to three months. Allow to defrost overnight in the fridge. Reheat in a saucepan for about 10 minutes, stir in the cream and heat until piping hot and serve as above.

# Grilled aubergine, red onion and raspberries   *See Page 99*

There are lots of subtle tones of red and pink in garden vegetables and this salad mixes a few to give a wonderful display that is delicious to eat.

**Serves 4**

- 2 large pink or purple aubergines
- Salt
- 2 medium red onions, peeled
- 4 Tbsp raspberry vinegar (see page 80)
- 6 Tbsp light olive oil
- 1 tsp cumin seeds, lightly crushed
- 1 tsp coriander seeds, lightly crushed
- Freshly ground black pepper
- 1 Tbsp clear honey
- 1 Tbsp wholegrain mustard
- 1 small radicchio lettuce
- Small bunch purple basil
- 225 g (8 oz) fresh raspberries

**1** Preheat the oven to 200° C (400° F / gas 6). Trim the ends off the aubergines and cut into thin round slices. Stand a colander or large sieve in a bowl and layer up the aubergine slices, sprinkling with salt as you go. Set aside for 30 minutes, then rinse well, drain and pat dry with kitchen paper.

**2** Meanwhile, halve the onions and cut into thick wedges. Separate the layers and place in a small glass or china bowl. Toss in 1 tablespoon of the vinegar and set aside.

**3** Line a large baking sheet with baking parchment and arrange the aubergine and onion slices on top. Drizzle with 4 tablespoons of oil and sprinkle with the seeds and black pepper. Bake in the oven for about 30 minutes, turning occasionally, until tender and golden. Drain well and keep warm.

**4** In a small bowl, whisk the remaining vinegar and oil together with the honey, mustard and some seasoning to make a dressing. Set aside until ready to serve.

**5** When ready to serve, break up the radicchio and remove the core. Rinse and shake off the excess water. Break up the leaves and arrange on serving plates. Sprinkle with a few basil leaves, top with the warm aubergine and onion and a few raspberries. Drizzle the dressing over each portion and serve.

❄ **FREEZING**  Not suitable

**COOK'S NOTE**  For a main meal salad try adding cooked chicken to the dish or pieces of buffalo mozzarella.

# Fresh bean minestrone with rocket pesto *See Page 100*

For their stunning bright green colour, I like to peel the broad beans for this soup. Of course, this is time consuming and a bit wasteful, but for older, bigger beans it makes them more palatable. If you don't want to do this, simply cook them in the soup with the other beans.

**Serves 4**

**For the minestrone**

- 675 g (1 lb 8 oz) broad beans, shelled
- 25 g (1 oz) butter
- 1 large onion, peeled and finely chopped
- 1 garlic clove, peeled and crushed
- 1 large carrot, peeled and finely diced
- 1 stick celery, trimmed and finely chopped
- 1.2 l (40 fl oz) chicken or vegetable stock
- 50 g (2 oz) spaghetti
- 225 g (8 oz) runner beans, trimmed and sliced
- 115 g (4 oz) French beans, topped and tailed and cut into 2.5 cm (1 in) lengths
- 8 ripe plum tomatoes, skinned, filleted and chopped (see page 94), or 200 g (7 oz) tin chopped tomatoes

**For the pesto**

- 1 garlic clove, peeled and chopped
- 15 g (½ oz) fresh rocket
- 100 g (3½ oz) pine nuts, lightly toasted
- 60 g (2 oz) finely grated fresh pecorino cheese
- 4 Tbsp extra virgin olive oil

1 Start by making the minestrone. Bring a small saucepan of water to the boil and cook the broad beans for 4 to 6 minutes until tender. Drain well and rinse under cold running water to cool. Peel off the skins and set aside.

2 In a large saucepan, melt the butter until bubbling and then add the onion, garlic, carrot and celery, and gently fry for 5 to 6 minutes until the onion is softened but not browned. Pour in the stock and bring to the boil. Break the spaghetti into short lengths and add to the stock, bring back to the boil and add the runner and French beans, and simmer for 10 to 15 minutes until the pasta and beans are tender.

3 Meanwhile, make the pesto. Place all the ingredients in a blender or food processor and blend for a few seconds until smooth. Cover and set aside until required.

4 Stir the chopped tomatoes and broad beans into the soup and cook for a further 2 minutes to heat through. Ladle into warm serving bowls and serve each with a dollop of pesto on top.

**FREEZING** Make the soup as above but omit the pesto. Allow to cool, then pack into freezer soup bags or a freezer-proof container. Seal, label and freeze for up to three months. Allow to defrost overnight in the fridge. Reheat in a saucepan for about 15 minutes until piping hot. Make the pesto and serve as above.

# Warm Turkish-style baby carrot salad  *See Page 101*

Tender sweet baby carrots are best for this recipe but if you prefer, just cut larger ones into strips or thin wedges. Cook gently to release the full sweetness, and serve with warm pitta bread, homemade tzatziki and humous.

*Serves 4*

### For the carrot salad

- 450 g (1 lb) baby carrots
- 2 Tbsp olive oil
- ½ tsp cumin seeds
- Juice of ½ lemon
- 2 tsp caster sugar
- ½ tsp sweet paprika
- 2 Tbsp freshly chopped coriander

### For the tzatziki

- ¼ medium cucumber, finely chopped
- 2 Tbsp freshly chopped mint
- 200 ml (7 fl oz) natural Greek or whole milk yoghurt
- Salt and freshly ground black pepper

- Pitta bread, to serve

1 Scrub the carrots and top and tail them. Heat the oil in a frying pan and add the carrots and cumin seeds. Stir for about 1 minute, then leave to cook over a low heat, turning occasionally, for 15 to 20 minutes, until tender and lightly golden.

2 Meanwhile, make the tzatziki. Mix the cucumber and mint into the yoghurt, season well, then cover and chill until required.

3 Turn the carrots and juices into a warm serving dish and toss in the lemon juice, sugar, paprika and seasoning. Mix well, cover and stand for 10 minutes. Serve the carrots warm sprinkled with chopped coriander and accompanied with tzatziki and warm pitta bread.

❀ **FREEZING**  Not suitable

**COOK'S NOTE**  For a flavour variation, try cooking strips of parsnip and sweet potato along with carrot. Even new potatoes taste great with this spicy dressing.

# Chilled cucumber soup

A delicately coloured soup that is rich and flavoursome. Ideal as a cooler on a summer's evening. Can also be served in small cups or glasses as part of a canapé tray.

*Serves 4–6*

- 2 Tbsp light olive oil
- 1 large onion, peeled and finely chopped
- 2 garlic cloves, peeled and crushed
- 1 bay leaf
- 1 large cucumber, peeled and chopped
- 600 ml (1 pint) chicken or vegetable stock
- 50 g (2 oz) ground almonds
- 6 Tbsp whole milk natural yoghurt
- Salt and freshly ground black pepper
- 2 Tbsp freshly chopped dill
- Cucumber slices and ice cubes, to serve

1 Heat the oil in a medium saucepan and gently fry the onion and garlic with the bay leaf for 10 minutes until soft but not browned.

2 Stir in the cucumber and pour over the stock. Bring to the boil, then cover and simmer gently for 10 minutes. Remove from the heat and set aside to cool. Discard the bay leaf.

3 Transfer to a blender or food processor and whiz for a few seconds until smooth. Stir in the ground almonds and yoghurt to thicken, then taste to season. Allow to cool, then cover and chill for at least 2 hours. Stir in the chopped dill and serve with a few ice cubes and slices of cucumber to float.

**FREEZING** Make the soup but omit the yoghurt. Allow to cool, then pack into freezer soup bags or a freezer-proof container. Seal, label and freeze for up to three months. Allow to defrost overnight in the fridge. Stir in the yoghurt and chopped dill and serve as above.

# Fennel salad with prawns and Pernod

Crisp textures and simple flavours make up this very refreshing salad. I like the 'bite' of chopped spring onion sprinkled over, but you may wish to leave this out for a less robust flavour.

**Serves 4**

- 2 bulbs fennel
- I Tbsp lemon juice
- 3 medium oranges
- I cos lettuce or head of sweet romaine
- 350 g (12½ oz) peeled tiger prawns, thawed if frozen
- 2 Tbsp light olive oil
- 2 Tbsp Pernod
- Salt and freshly ground black pepper
- 2 spring onions, trimmed and finely chopped (optional)

**I** Trim the fennel, reserving the green fronds for garnish, and slice the bulbs very thinly. Sprinkle with lemon juice and place in a shallow dish. Set aside.

**2** Using a sharp knife, slice the top and bottom off the oranges and slice off the peel taking away as much of the white pith as possible. Cut into thin, round slices and arrange over the fennel slices. Cover and chill for I hour.

**3** When ready to serve, break the lettuce into small pieces and rinse well. Shake off the excess water and arrange on serving plates. Drain the fennel and orange slices from the dish, reserving the orange juice, and arrange on top of the lettuce. Wash and pat dry the prawns and add some to each serving. Place the reserved orange juice in a small bowl and whisk in the olive oil, Pernod and seasoning. Drizzle over each portion and serve sprinkled with a few chopped spring onions, if using, and the reserved fennel fronds.

❄ **FREEZING** Not suitable

**COOK'S NOTE** If you would rather not use Pernod, then either grind a little star anise or a few aniseeds and sprinkle over the salad to season it, or you could add a pinch of Chinese five spice powder.

# Alsace onion tart

Traditionally this German speciality is made with a white bread dough base, so the finished result is more like a pizza than a tart. I prefer to use puff pastry as a base.

### Serves 4–6

• 50 g (2 oz) butter

• 2 large onions, peeled and thinly sliced

• 2 garlic cloves, peeled and crushed

• 250 g (9 oz) puff pastry, thawed if frozen

• 1 large egg yolk

• 3 Tbsp soured cream

• ¼ tsp ground nutmeg

• Salt and freshly ground black pepper

• 1 tsp caraway seeds, lightly crushed

1 Preheat the oven to 200° C (400° F / gas 6). Melt the butter in a large frying pan and gently fry the onions and garlic for about 15 minutes, stirring occasionally, until tender and golden brown.

2 Meanwhile, roll out the pastry on a lightly floured surface to form a 25 cm (10 in) square. Prick all over with a fork and bake in the oven to 10 to 12 minutes to 'set' and lightly brown.

3 Mix the egg yolk, soured cream and nutmeg together, and season well. Carefully brush all over the pastry and spread out the cooked onions on top. Sprinkle with caraway seeds and bake for a further 10 minutes until golden and crisp. Best served warm.

**FREEZING** Allow to cool completely and either leave whole or cut in slices. Open freeze on a tray lined with baking parchment, then wrap well. Store for up to three months. Reheat on a baking tray from frozen in the oven at 200° C (400° F / gas 6) for 20 to 25 minutes until piping hot.

# Pea cakes and pea shoot salad See Page 102

Not only do peas taste good but they certainly brighten up the plate! Snip a few of the young shoots off, too, and throw into a salad mix for a lovely sweet 'pea' flavour.

**Serves 4**

- 625 g (1 lb 6 oz) fresh peas, shelled (approx. 300 g / 10½ oz shelled weight)
- Salt
- 2 tsp caster sugar
- 115 g (4 oz) gram (chick pea) flour
- 50 g (2 oz) fine cornmeal
- 2 tsp baking powder
- 1 medium egg, separated
- 300 ml (½ pint) whole milk
- 50 g (2 oz) butter, melted
- 1 Tbsp vegetable oil
- 8 rashers rindless streaky bacon
- Handful of fresh pea shoots, rinsed
- 4 Tbsp crème fraîche

**1** Bring a small saucepan of lightly salted water to the boil. Add the peas and 1 teaspoon of sugar, then cover and cook for about 10 minutes until just tender. Drain well. Reserve half the cooked peas and, using a potato masher or fork, mash the remaining peas.

**2** Sieve the flour, cornmeal, baking powder and remaining sugar into a bowl. Make a well in the centre and add the egg yolk, pea purée and milk. Carefully whisk into the dry ingredients to form a thick batter. In a separate bowl, whisk the egg white until foamy but not too stiff and fold into the batter along with the whole peas.

**3** Keeping half the butter to one side, heat a little of the remaining butter with a little of the oil in a large frying pan until bubbling and ladle 2 tablespoon portions of batter into the pan, leaving space for the cakes to expand. Cook over a low to moderate heat for about 2 minutes on each side until golden. Drain, cover and keep warm whilst using up all the batter to make approximately 16 pea cakes, buttering and oiling the pan as necessary and stirring the batter to redistribute the peas each time before using.

**4** Melt the remaining butter until bubbling and cook the bacon for 2 to 3 minutes on each side until cooked through and crisp. Drain on kitchen paper and keep warm until ready to serve.

**5** To serve, arrange a few pea shoots on serving plates. Top with pea cakes and add a dollop of crème fraîche. Cut the bacon into small pieces and sprinkle over the top. Serve warm.

**FREEZING** Allow the pea cakes to cool and stack between layers of baking parchment. Place the stack in a freezer bag and seal well. Freeze for up to three months. Allow to thaw overnight in the refrigerator. To reheat, divide into two stacks and place on a baking sheet lined with baking parchment. Cover with foil and place in a preheated oven at 190° C (375° F / gas 5) for about 8 minutes until piping hot. Proceed with the recipe above.

# Spinach roulade with sweet pepper

This makes an attractive starter and is surprisingly simple to make. Work with the spinach base whilst it is still warm and malleable, and don't be too worried if it cracks.

**Serves 6**

- 4 large red peppers
- 450 g (1 lb) baby spinach leaves
- 4 large eggs, separated
- ½ tsp ground nutmeg
- Salt and freshly ground black pepper
- 25 g (1 oz) freshly grated Parmesan cheese
- 400 g (14 oz) low fat soft cheese with garlic and herbs
- 4 Tbsp freshly chopped parsley

1 Preheat the oven to 220° C (425° F / gas 7). Grease and line a 32 x 23 cm (13 x 9 in) Swiss roll tin. Line a small baking sheet with baking parchment.

2 Halve the peppers and remove the seeds. Cut in half again and place on the small baking sheet. Bake in the oven, turning occasionally, for about 25 minutes, until tender and lightly charred. Cool for 20 minutes, then peel off the skin. Cut the pepper flesh into thin strips and set aside.

3 Meanwhile, rinse the spinach in a colander or large sieve and pack into a large saucepan whilst still wet. Cover with a tight-fitting lid and cook over a medium heat for 5 to 6 minutes until wilted. Drain thoroughly, squeezing out as much liquid as possible. Chop finely and pat dry using kitchen paper.

4 Place the spinach in a bowl and mix in the egg yolks, nutmeg and seasoning. In a separate bowl, whisk the egg whites until very frothy but not stiff, and fold into the spinach mixture. Spread the mixture into the prepared tin and bake for 12 to 15 minutes until just firm and lightly golden.

5 Sprinkle the Parmesan evenly over a sheet of baking parchment slightly larger than the size of the spinach base. Turn the cooked base on to the paper and peel away the lining paper. Carefully spread over the soft cheese and arrange the cooked pepper slices on top. Sprinkle with chopped parsley.

6 Working quickly and using the parchment as a guide, start at one of the short ends and tightly roll up the base like a Swiss roll. Serve sliced, hot or cold.

**FREEZING** The roulade base will freeze. Simply cool in the tin, wrap well in parchment, clear wrap and then foil, and freeze in the tin. Store for up to three months. Allow to defrost overnight in the tin and wrapping. To reheat, preheat the oven to 180° C (350° F / gas 4), discard the freezer wrapping, and cover with foil. Place the tin in the oven for about 15 minutes, then continue as above.

# MAIN MEALS

## Apple, blue cheese and celery risotto   *See Page 103*

There's nothing complicated about making a risotto and this is one of the simplest to make. Try replacing the apple with cubed squash or pumpkin when they are in season.

**Serves 4**
- 350 g (12½ oz) cooking apples
- 150 ml (5 fl oz) unsweetened apple juice
- 1.2 l (40 fl oz) vegetable stock
- 50 g (2 oz) butter
- 1 medium onion, peeled and finely chopped
- 2 sticks celery, trimmed and finely chopped
- 400 g (14 oz) Arborio rice
- 150 g (5½ oz) blue cheese such as Stilton, Roquefort or Gorgonzola
- Salt and freshly ground black pepper
- A few celery leaves, roughly chopped

**1** Peel, core and cut the apples into small pieces. Place in a saucepan with the apple juice, bring to the boil, then cover and cook for 1 to 2 minutes until just tender but not collapsed. Drain and set aside, reserving the liquid to make up the stock.

**2** Pour the stock into a saucepan and bring to the boil. Stir in the reserved cooking liquid and reduce to a gentle simmer.

**3** Meanwhile, melt the butter in a large saucepan and gently fry the onion and celery for 2 to 3 minutes until softened but not browned. Stir in the rice and cook, stirring, for 2 minutes, until well coated. Add a ladleful of stock and cook gently, stirring, until absorbed. Continue adding the stock, ladle by ladle, to the rice until half the stock is used and the rice is creamy.

**4** Add the remaining stock and stir occasionally until the risotto becomes thick but not sticky. This will take about 25 minutes and should not be hurried. Just before serving, crumble the cheese into the rice and fold in along with the cooked apple. Season and serve immediately, sprinkled with the chopped celery leaves.

**COOK'S NOTE** This basic risotto recipe can be used as a base for other versions. Simply replace the apple and celery with other lightly cooked vegetables such as peas, beans, sweet corn and courgette.

**FREEZING** Follow the recipe above but omit the cheese. Allow to cool, then pack into a rigid container. Keep for up to three months. Defrost in the fridge overnight and reheat gently in a saucepan, adding a little more liquid as necessary, until piping hot. Add the cheese before serving.

# Melanzane alla parmigiana

This is my favourite vegetarian recipe of all time. Aubergines cook to a meltingly tender consistency in this dish and they are surprisingly 'meaty'. It is very rich, so I have kept the portion sizes open to suit personal taste.

**Serves 4–6**
- 900 g (2 lb) pink, purple or white aubergines, or any combination
- Salt
- Approximately 150 ml (5 fl oz) good quality olive oil
- 1 large red onion, peeled and finely chopped
- 1 garlic clove, peeled and finely chopped
- 1 quantity Fresh tomato sauce (see page 94)
- 115 g (4 oz) freshly grated Parmesan cheese
- Salad and bread, to serve

1 Preheat the oven to 180° C (350° F / gas 4). Trim the aubergines and cut into lengthways slices about 2 cm (¾ in) thick. Layer the slices in a colander, sprinkling with salt as you go. Place the colander in a bowl and set aside for 30 minutes.

2 Meanwhile, heat 1 tablespoon of oil and gently fry the onion and garlic for about 15 minutes until softened but not browned. Set aside.

3 Once the aubergines are ready, rinse well in cold water and pat dry using kitchen paper. In a large frying pan heat 2 to 3 tablespoons of oil and fry a few slices of aubergine for 2 minutes on each side until lightly golden. Drain well on kitchen paper. Repeat, using the oil as needed to fry the remaining slices, draining each batch on kitchen paper.

4 Add the cooked onion mixture into the tomato sauce and spoon one third into the base of a shallow 2-litre (64-fl oz) gratin dish. Lay half the aubergine slices neatly on top and spoon over half the remaining sauce. Top with the remaining aubergine slices and spread over the rest of the sauce. Sprinkle with the cheese and place the dish on a baking sheet. Bake in the oven for about 50 minutes until tender, golden and bubbling. Stand for 10 minutes before serving with a salad and some bread to mop up the sauce.

**COOK'S NOTE** If you haven't got time to make your own tomato sauce, you can use 600 ml (1 pint) ready-made passata or sieved cooked tomatoes and add some chopped herbs of choice for extra flavouring.

**FREEZING** Allow to cool and either leave whole (make sure the dish is freezer-proof) or divide into portions and pack into rigid containers. Keep for up to three months. Defrost in the fridge overnight. Reheat, covered with foil, at 200° C (400° F / gas 6), for 20 to 30 minutes, depending on the size of the portion, until piping hot.

# Roast salmon with green bean salsa  *See Page 104*

A vibrant combination of fresh flavours to go with this favourite of fishes. The bean salsa can also be cooled and chilled, and served as a salad.

*Serves 4*

- 4 x 175 g (6 oz) salmon fillets
- Salt and freshly ground black pepper
- 3 Tbsp light olive oil
- 2 tsp coriander seeds, lightly crushed
- 1 tsp fennel seeds, lightly crushed
- 675 g (1 lb 8 oz) broad beans, shelled
- 225 g (8 oz) French beans, topped, tailed and cut into 2.5 cm (1 in) lengths
- ¼ cucumber, diced
- 1 small green pepper, deseeded and diced
- 4 spring onions, trimmed and chopped
- 2 Tbsp white wine vinegar
- 2 tsp caster sugar
- 2 Tbsp freshly chopped dill
- Lemon wedges, to serve

1 Preheat the oven to 200° C (400° F / gas 6). Wash and pat dry the salmon. Season all over and place on a baking tray lined with baking parchment. Drizzle lightly with 1 tablespoon of oil and sprinkle with the crushed seeds. Bake in the oven for 15 to 20 minutes, depending on thickness, until just cooked through. Drain and keep warm.

2 Bring a saucepan of lightly salted water to the boil and cook the beans together, covered, for 4 to 6 minutes until just cooked. Drain well and rinse in cold running water to cool. Drain again and pat dry with kitchen paper.

3 Turn the beans into a bowl and mix in the cucumber, pepper and spring onions. Mix the remaining olive oil with the vinegar, sugar, dill and some seasoning, and toss into the vegetables.

4 To serve, pile the salsa onto serving plates and top with a piece of salmon. Serve with wedges of lemon to squeeze over.

❋ **FREEZING**  Not suitable

**COOK'S NOTE**  You can turn the salsa into a light meal by frying off 225 g (8 oz) diced pancetta or bacon and tossing into the mixture. Serve with a handful of wild rocket or baby salad leaves.

# Peppered steak with fried cabbage and turnip chips

This is the type of meal that reminds me of food served in rural French bistros. Not the most colourful of combinations but a really great mixture of peppery flavours.

**Serves 4**

- 450 g (1 lb) small white turnips such as Milan
- Salt and freshly ground black pepper
- 75 g (2½ oz) butter
- 1 Tbsp light brown sugar
- 4 x 150 g (5½ oz) fillet steaks
- 1 Tbsp pink peppercorns (dry)
- 1 Tbsp black peppercorns
- 1 Tbsp olive oil
- 150 ml (5 fl oz) whole milk
- Approximately 115 g (4 oz) plain flour
- 450 g (1 lb) firm white cabbage, trimmed, core removed and cut into 1 cm (½ in) thick shreds
- Sunflower oil, for deep frying
- 4 Tbsp freshly chopped parsley

**1** Peel the turnips and cut into small chip shapes about 1 cm (½ in) thick. Place in a saucepan, add a pinch of salt and cover with water. Bring to the boil and cook for 6 to 7 minutes, until just tender. Drain well.

**2** Melt 50 g (2 oz) butter in a frying pan and stir in the sugar until it dissolves. Add the turnips, tossing them well in the butter, and cook over a medium heat, stirring occasionally, for 8 to 10 minutes, until golden and caramelised. Drain well and keep warm.

**3** Meanwhile, rinse and pat dry the steaks. Crush the pink and black peppercorns together using a pestle and mortar and press on to both sides of the steak. Melt the remaining butter with the olive oil until bubbling and frothy, lower to a medium heat and cook the steaks for 3 to 4 minutes on each side for rare, 5 to 6 minutes for medium, and about 7 minutes on each side for well done. Drain and keep warm.

**4** To prepare the cabbage, pour the milk into a bowl and put 3 tablespoons of the flour on a sheet of greaseproof paper and season well. Dip a few shreds of cabbage in the milk, then toss them in the flour. Heat the oil for deep frying to 190° C (375° F) and fry a few shreds at a time for about 2 minutes until golden and crisp. Drain on kitchen paper and keep warm whilst preparing the remaining cabbage, adding more flour to the paper as necessary.

**5** To serve, pile the cabbage and turnips on to warmed serving plates and top with a piece of steak. Sprinkle with chopped parsley and serve.

❄ **FREEZING** Not suitable

**COOK'S NOTE** Serve the cabbage as soon as you can after frying as it will lose its crispiness on standing; this recipe is also good with red cabbage. If small turnips are unavailable, use larger ones and cut them into small pieces.

# Roast lamb and garlic with celeriac mash *See Page 105*

This is a very rich flavoursome dish, and the garlic cooks to a sweet tenderness that is excellent served with rich lamb and this gourmet mash.

**Serves 6**

**For the lamb**

- 1.35 kg (3 lb) half leg of lamb
- Salt and freshly ground black pepper
- 1 tsp each of cumin, coriander and fennel seeds, lightly crushed
- 2 Tbsp olive oil
- 6 whole garlic bulbs, white papery skin removed
- 3 Tbsp redcurrant jelly
- 300 ml (½ pint) chicken stock

**For the celeriac mash**

- 450 g (1 lb) mashing potatoes such as Maris Piper or King Edward
- 450 g (1 lb) celeriac
- 50 g (2 oz) butter
- 4 Tbsp milk or double cream
- 1 tsp toasted fennel seeds, lightly crushed

1 Start by preparing the lamb. Preheat the oven to 180° C (350° F / gas 4). Trim away the excess fat from the lamb, then wash, pat dry and season all over. Press the crushed seeds into the lamb flesh.

2 Heat the oil in a large frying pan and fry the lamb for about 10 minutes, turning frequently, until golden brown all over. Transfer the lamb and juices to a large ovenproof casserole and set aside. Arrange the whole garlic around the lamb, cover with a layer of foil, then set the lid on top. Bake in the oven for about 2 hours until tender.

3 Meanwhile, make the mash. Peel the potatoes and celeriac and cut into small chunks. Place in a large saucepan and cover with water. Add a pinch of salt and bring to the boil. Cook for about 10 minutes until tender. Drain well through a colander or sieve and stand for 10 minutes to dry before returning to the saucepan. Mash well and stir in the butter and milk or cream – for a really smooth mash, put the mixture through a vegetable ricer. Adjust the seasoning and pile into a warmed serving dish. Cover and keep warm.

4 Drain the lamb and garlic, reserving the cooking juices, and place on a warmed serving platter. Cover loosely with foil and stand for 10 minutes. Strain the cooking juices into a saucepan and add the redcurrant jelly and stock, and heat gently until melted, then raise the heat and boil for 3 to 4 minutes until slightly reduced and syrupy. Serve with the lamb. Sprinkle the mash with toasted fennel seeds and black pepper.

❄ **FREEZING** Not suitable

# Baked herb chicken with fondant potatoes

A fragrant way to cook a chicken enhanced with light herbs and celery. The potatoes are to die for, and you may think on first glance that two per person isn't enough, but they are very rich and indulgent.

*Serves 4*

- 1.35 kg (3 lb) oven-ready free range chicken
- Salt and freshly ground black pepper
- 250 g (9 oz) lightly salted butter, softened
- 4 bay leaves
- Small bunch fresh tarragon
- 2 stalks celery with leaves
- 1 small lemon, halved
- 8 small waxy potatoes such as Charlotte or Nadine, about the size of a large chicken's egg (about 675 g / 1 lb 8 oz in weight)
- Fresh tarragon, to garnish

1 Preheat the oven to 190° C (375° F / gas 5). Rinse and pat dry the chicken inside and out. Season well inside. Starting at the tip of the breastbone, loosen the skin away from the chicken flesh, carefully snipping with a pair of kitchen scissors as necessary. Loosen the skin right down to the wishbone and over the legs, taking care not to tear it.

2 Carefully butter the chicken flesh with 50 g (2 oz) butter and arrange the bay leaves over the flesh, then push in the tarragon leaves. Slice off the celery leaves from the stalks and push in between the flesh and skin. Gently smooth the skin back down over the flesh. Roughly chop the celery stalks and place inside the bird, along with the halved lemon.

3 Stand the chicken in a roasting tin and season the outside. Bake in the oven for about 1½ hours, basting occasionally, until the juices from the centre run clear. Drain and place on a warm serving platter. Cover loosely with foil and stand for 10 minutes before carving.

4 Whilst the chicken is cooking, trim the potatoes into barrel shapes using a peeler or paring knife, and take a slice off the top and bottom of each. Melt the remaining butter in a medium saucepan over a low heat – you need to use a pan in which the potatoes fit snugly and the melted butter comes at least halfway up the sides of the potatoes. Lower the potatoes into the pan and cook for about 50 minutes, turning over halfway through, until a skewer inserted into the centre of the potato meets little resistance. Drain, season lightly and keep warm.

5 To serve, arrange the fondant potatoes around the chicken and garnish with fresh tarragon. For extra indulgence, spoon over some of the melted butter from cooking the potatoes.

❄ **FREEZING** Not suitable

# Corned beef, neeps and tattie pie

Pure comfort food; this pie is full of satisfying root vegetables encased in pastry. If you're vegetarian, you can easily leave out the beef and add more vegetables or grated Cheddar cheese.

**Serves 6**
- 500 g (1 lb 2 oz) shortcrust pastry, thawed if frozen
- 1 small onion, peeled and finely chopped
- 225 g (8 oz) swede, peeled and coarsely grated
- 225 g (8 oz) turnips, peeled and coarsely grated
- 225 g (8 oz) potatoes, peeled and coarsely grated
- Salt and freshly ground black pepper
- 350 g (12½ oz) corned beef or haggis
- 1 medium egg, beaten, to glaze

1 Preheat the oven to 200° C (400° F / gas 6). Roll out just over half the pastry on a lightly floured surface to fit a 20 cm (8 in) round pie dish or tin, 5 cm (2 in) deep. Cover and chill until required.

2 Put the onion in a bowl and mix in the grated vegetables. Season well. On a plate, mash the corned beef or haggis to an even texture.

3 Press the vegetables into the pastry case and top with corned beef. Roll out the remaining pastry to make a lid. Brush the edge of the pastry case with beaten egg and seal the lid on top, pressing the edge all round with the prongs of a fork. Make two small slits in the middle of the lid, brush all over with egg and place on a baking sheet. Bake for 30 minutes until golden, then reduce the oven temperature to 180° C (350° F / gas 4) and cook the pie for a further 30 minutes or so until the vegetables are tender and the pastry is golden brown. Serve hot with onion gravy (see page 156) or cold with a salad.

**COOK'S NOTE** This traditional pie is equally as good made with grated beetroot, parsnip, celeriac, carrot or Jerusalem artichoke, and you can replace the onion with chopped leeks, spring onion or chives.

**FREEZING** Cool and leave whole making sure the pie dish is freezer proof or cut into portions and pack into rigid containers. Wrap well and keep for up to three months. Defrost in the fridge overnight. Reheat covered in foil at 200° C (400° F / gas 6) for 20 to 35 minutes depending on size, until piping hot.

# Venison with blackberry sauce  *See Page 106*

This dish has a distinctly autumnal feel about it. The blackberry sauce would work equally well with fillet steak or pheasant.

### Serves 4

- 4 venison steaks
- Salt and freshly ground black pepper
- 1 Tbsp juniper berries, crushed
- 25 g (1 oz) unsalted butter
- 1 shallot, peeled and finely chopped
- 225 g (8 oz) blackberries, rinsed and hulled
- 2 Tbsp ruby port
- 2 Tbsp blackberry or raspberry vinegar (see page 80)
- 2 Tbsp redcurrant jelly
- 2 Tbsp freshly chopped parsley

1 Rinse and pat dry the venison pieces. Season on both sides with salt, pepper and juniper, rubbing in the seasoning. Cover and chill for 30 minutes.

2 Melt the butter in a frying pan until bubbling and cook the venison for about 4 to 5 minutes on each side – this will cook the steaks to medium. Drain, reserving the pan juices, and keep warm.

3 Gently fry the shallot for 5 minutes in the reserved juices until softened. Stir in the blackberries and port, bring to the boil, and cover and simmer for 5 minutes until softened. Stir in the vinegar and redcurrant jelly and heat gently until melted.

4 To serve, spoon the blackberries and sauce over each medallion and sprinkle with chopped parsley. Delicious accompanied with Classic potato dauphinoise (see page 160) or celeriac mash (see page 143).

**FREEZING** The sauce is suitable for freezing. Allow to cool, then transfer to a rigid container. Seal and freeze for up to six months. Defrost in the fridge overnight and reheat in a saucepan until piping hot.

# Stir-fried pork with broccoli and cucumber  *See Page 107*

You don't have to save cucumber for salads or pickles; it makes an unusual addition to a stir-fry. It's lovely with chicken or fish too.

**Serves 4**

- ½ cucumber
- 2 tsp salt
- 225 g (8 oz) broccoli
- 1 Tbsp sunflower oil
- 450 g (1 lb) lean pork
- 2 garlic cloves, peeled and crushed
- 1 Tbsp light soy sauce
- 1 Tbsp Chinese cooking wine or sweet sherry
- 2 Tbsp freshly chopped chives
- Noodles, to serve

1 Peel the cucumber using a vegetable peeler. Halve it lengthways and scrape out the seeds with a teaspoon. Cut into 2.5 cm (1 in) thick diagonal slices and place in a nylon sieve over a bowl. Toss in the salt and set aside for 30 minutes.

2 Meanwhile, cut the broccoli into small florets or pieces, and slice the pork into thin strips. Cover and chill until required.

3 Rinse the cucumber well and pat dry with kitchen paper. Heat the oil in a wok or large frying pan and stir-fry the pork and garlic for 5 minutes. Add the soy sauce, wine or sherry, cucumber and broccoli and stir-fry for a further 4 to 5 minutes until the vegetables are just tender and the pork is cooked through. Sprinkle with chives and serve immediately with freshly cooked noodles.

❄ **FREEZING**  Not suitable

**COOK'S NOTE**  Other good combinations with cucumber would be slices or strips of courgette, mange-tout or sugar snap peas, or green beans.

# Cauliflower biriyani with sweet carrot relish *See Page 108*

Using whole spices really is worth the effort and gives a great flavour. For an alternative version, replace the spices with 1 tablespoon of good quality fragrant curry paste.

**Serves 4**

- 3 Tbsp sunflower oil
- 6 cardamom pods, crushed
- 1 tsp cumin seeds, lightly crushed
- 1 tsp coriander seeds, lightly crushed
- 1 small cinnamon stick, broken
- 1 medium onion, peeled and chopped
- 1½ tsp ground turmeric
- 1 bay leaf
- 175 g (6 oz) basmati rice, rinsed
- 50 g (2 oz) red lentils, rinsed
- 600 ml (1 pint) vegetable stock
- 1 small cauliflower, cut into small florets or pieces
- Salt and freshly ground black pepper
- 1 large carrot, peeled and coarsely grated
- 2 tsp caster sugar
- 50 g (2 oz) sultanas
- 1 tsp black onion seeds (optional)
- 4 Tbsp freshly chopped coriander

1 Heat 1 tablespoon of oil in a large saucepan and stir-fry the cardamom, cumin and coriander seeds and cinnamon for 1 minute until lightly fragrant, then add the onion and fry, stirring, for about 5 minutes until softened, but not browned.

2 Add the turmeric, bay leaf, rice and lentils, and cook for a further minute, stirring, to coat the rice in the spice mixture. Pour over the stock and bring to the boil. Add the cauliflower, cover and simmer gently for 15 minutes, stirring occasionally, until the rice is tender. Remove from the heat and stand covered for 10 minutes to allow the stock to absorb. Discard the bay leaf, cinnamon stick and cardamom pods. Season to taste.

3 Meanwhile, make the carrot relish. Heat the remaining oil until hot and stir-fry the grated carrot for 2 minutes until just wilting. Add the sugar and sultanas and stir-fry for a further 2 to 3 minutes until lightly golden. Stir in the onion seeds if using.

4 To serve, pile the cauliflower rice on to warm serving plates and top with some carrot relish. Sprinkle with fresh coriander and serve immediately.

**COOK'S NOTE** You can add a variety of vegetables to this dish; try carrot, broccoli, broad beans, sugar snap peas or cubed squash.

**FREEZING** The rice part of this recipe is suitable for freezing. Allow to cool, then pack into a rigid container. Seal and freeze for up to three months. Defrost in the fridge overnight. Reheat by putting in a large saucepan with a little water. Heat gently and when steaming, cover and cook, stirring occasionally, until piping hot. Prepare the carrot relish as above and serve with the rice.

# ACCOMPANIMENTS

## Beetroot in raspberry jelly

This might sound a bit weird but it really is delicious! It's based on a recipe given to my mum by a friend who makes it with blackcurrant jelly. It's always a talking point and makes an excellent accompaniment to thickly sliced ham or smoked chicken.

**Serves 8–10**

- 450 g (1 lb) young raw beetroot, each weighing about 90 g (3 oz)
- 135 g (5 oz) packet raspberry jelly
- 300 ml (½ pint) raspberry vinegar (see page 80)
- 2 medium red onions, peeled and very finely chopped or grated

1 Trim the leaf stalks from the beetroot, and leave the root intact. Place in a saucepan and cover with lightly salted water. Bring to the boil and cook for about 1½ hours. Drain and rinse under cold running water until cool enough to handle, then carefully rub off the skins. Allow to cool completely, then chop into small pieces.

2 Meanwhile, make up the jelly according to the packet instructions, replacing half the water with the vinegar and allow to cool.

3 Mix the beetroot and onions together and pack into a 450 g (1 lb) loaf tin. Pour over the jelly and chill for at least 2 hours until set.

4 To serve, dip the tin in hot water for a few seconds to loosen, then invert on to a serving plate. Serve in slices as part of a salad – it will crumble, so you may prefer to use a spoon to scoop up the jelly.

**Variation:** Try setting grated carrot and chopped raw leek in an orange jelly made up with half water and half freshly squeezed orange juice.

❄ **FREEZING** Not suitable

# Stir-fried Brussels sprouts with pancetta *See Page 109*

You can prepare the various elements of this dish in advance, but the cooking has to be done at the last minute in order to retain the sweetness of the sprouts. This combination also works well for shredded cabbage or small florets of broccoli.

**Serves 4**

- 2 Tbsp sunflower oil
- 25 g (1 oz) unsalted butter
- 50 g (2 oz) fresh white breadcrumbs
- 450 g (1 lb) small Brussels sprouts
- 150 g (5½ oz) diced pancetta (or fatty bacon)
- 2 Tbsp freshly grated Parmesan cheese

1 Heat the oil in a frying pan with the butter until melted and frothy. Add the breadcrumbs and stir-fry for 2 to 3 minutes until richly golden. Drain on kitchen paper and set aside.

2 Peel away the outer leaves from the sprouts. Quarter the sprouts and discard the outer leaves. If the sprouts are big, cut them into smaller pieces.

3 Put the pancetta in a frying pan and heat until the juices and fat start to melt. Add the Brussels sprouts and toss quickly in the pancetta fat. Stir-fry for 5 to 6 minutes until the sprouts are slightly softened. Toss in the breadcrumbs and heat through for a further minute. Serve immediately sprinkled with Parmesan.

❄ **FREEZING** Not suitable

**COOK'S NOTE** If you have the time, you can shred the sprouts and stir-fry them like shredded cabbage. Savoy cabbage would make a great alternative for non-sprout eaters!

# Crispy 'seaweed' and pak choi with oyster sauce

Forget the takeaway menu, these two classic oriental dishes are easy to make and delicious made with freshly picked vegetables.

**Serves 4**

**For the 'seaweed'**

• 450 g (1 lb) dark green cabbage such as Savoy, cavolo nero, spring greens or primo
• Vegetable oil for deep frying
• About 1 tsp salt
• About 1½ tsp caster sugar

**For the pak choi**

• 8 medium pak choi
• 1 Tbsp vegetable oil
• 1 garlic clove, peeled and crushed
• 1 small red chilli, deseeded and finely chopped (optional)
• 2 Tbsp oyster sauce
• 1 Tbsp dark soy sauce
• 2 tsp caster sugar

1 To prepare the 'seaweed', rinse and dry the cabbage and remove the tough stalks. Layer a few leaves on top of each other on a chopping board and roll up tightly, then using a sharp knife, slice very thinly into shreds.

2 Heat the oil for deep frying to 190° C (375° F) or until a few shreds of cabbage sizzle and crisp within 10 seconds. Place a small handful of cabbage in a deep frying basket and lower into the oil for a few seconds until crisp – the cabbage will hiss and bubble violently in the oil so take extra care. Drain well and keep warm whilst frying the remaining cabbage. Sprinkle with salt and sugar to taste. Best served warm, not hot.

3 To make the pak choi, rinse it and shake off the excess water. Cut in half lengthways and slice off the thicker stalk end. Heat the oil in a wok or large frying pan and stir-fry the garlic and chilli, if using, for 1 minute. Add the pak choi and stir-fry for a further minute. Add the sauces and sugar, and cook for 4 to 5 minutes until the pak choi is just tender. Serve immediately.

❄ **FREEZING** Not suitable

**COOK'S NOTE** Sprinkle the cabbage with toasted sesame seeds or chopped cashew nuts for extra bite. If you aren't using chilli in the pak choi recipe, you might like to sprinkle the finished dish with chopped spring onion or fresh chives.

# Sweet potato and spinach curry  *See Page 110*

A useful way of cooking root vegetables is to put them in a curry. Here I use sweet potatoes but white varieties work just as well, or you could try mixing in parsnip, turnip or carrot.

**Serves 4**

- 1 tsp coriander seeds, lightly crushed
- 1 tsp mustard seeds, lightly crushed
- 6 cardamom pods, green casing removed and seeds lightly crushed
- 1 onion, peeled and chopped
- 2 garlic cloves, peeled and chopped
- 2.5 cm (1 in) piece root ginger, peeled and chopped
- 2 fleshy mild green chillies, deseeded and chopped
- 2 Tbsp vegetable oil
- 675 g (1 lb 8 oz) sweet potatoes, peeled and cut into 2 cm (¾ in) thick pieces
- 400 ml (14 fl oz) tin coconut milk
- 1 tsp salt
- 225 g (8 oz) baby spinach, trimmed
- 4 Tbsp freshly chopped coriander

1 Dry fry the seeds and cardamom in a small frying pan, stirring for 3 to 4 minutes, until lightly toasted and fragrant. Set aside. Place the onion, garlic, ginger and chillies in a blender or food processor. Add the toasted spices and blend for a few seconds to make a paste.

2 Heat the oil in a large saucepan and gently fry the paste for 3 minutes until softened but not browned. Add the sweet potato and cook, stirring, for 1 minute until well coated in the paste.

3 Pour over the coconut milk and add the salt. Bring to the boil, then cover and simmer for 10 minutes until just tender. Stir in the spinach, cover and continue to cook for about 5 minutes, stirring occasionally, until the spinach is wilted and the potato is tender. Stir in the chopped coriander and serve as an accompaniment to other Indian-style dishes or grilled meat or chicken.

**FREEZING** Omit the spinach and chopped coriander. Allow to cool, then ladle into a rigid container. Seal well and freeze for up to three months. Defrost in the fridge overnight and reheat in a saucepan, stirring occasionally, until piping hot, stirring in the spinach towards the end of reheating as above.

# Cheesy cauliflower and broccoli fritters  *See Page 111*

An extra special accompaniment that's impressive when entertaining or makes a delicious addition to the Christmas table.

**Serves 4**

- 175 g (6 oz) cauliflower
- 175 g (6 oz) broccoli
- 50 g (2 oz) butter
- 50 g (2 oz) plain flour
- 600 ml (1 pint) whole milk
- 75 g (2½ oz) mature Cheddar cheese, grated
- ¼ tsp cayenne pepper
- ¼ tsp mustard powder
- Salt and freshly ground black pepper
- Vegetable oil for deep frying
- 115 g (4 oz) self-raising flour
- 1 medium egg, beaten

1 Cut the cauliflower and broccoli into florets or pieces about 2.5 cm (1 in) thick. Bring a saucepan of lightly salted water to the boil and cook the cauliflower and broccoli florets for about 5 minutes, until just tender. Drain well and leave to dry on a wire rack.

2 Meanwhile, melt the butter in a saucepan and stir in the plain flour. Cook for 1 minute then remove from the heat. Gradually blend in 450 ml (16 fl oz) of the milk, return to the heat and bring to the boil, stirring, until thickened. Cook for 1 minute. Remove from the heat and stir in the cheese, cayenne, mustard and seasoning.

3 Line a board with baking parchment. Dip each piece of cauliflower and broccoli in the warm sauce to coat completely and place on the paper. Leave aside to set, then chill for at least 2 hours.

4 Heat the oil for deep frying to 190° C (375° F). Whilst the oil is heating, sieve the self-raising flour into a bowl and make a well in the centre. Add the beaten egg, a pinch of salt and gradually whisk in the milk, blending the flour into the liquid as you go, to form a smooth thick batter – take care not to overwhisk.

5 When the oil has reached the correct temperature, dip individual pieces of cauliflower and broccoli in the batter and carefully lower into the oil. Cook in batches of about six pieces at a time for 4 to 5 minutes until crisp and golden. Drain well and keep warm whilst frying the other pieces. Serve immediately.

> **FREEZING**  Once cooked, allow to cool, then arrange on a tray lined with baking parchment. Open freeze, then pack into bags or rigid containers. Reheat from frozen at 200° C (400° F / gas 6) on a lined baking tray for about 20 to 25 minutes until crisp and piping hot.

# Braised celery

A tender and juicy way to enjoy the texture of cooked celery; an ideal accompaniment to roast or grilled chicken or fish.

**Serves 4**

- 2 heads celery
- 1 shallot or small onion, peeled and sliced
- 2 small carrots, peeled and chopped
- 300 ml (½ pint) chicken or vegetable stock
- Few sprigs fresh thyme
- Salt and freshly ground black pepper
- 25 g (1 oz) unsalted butter, softened
- 25 g (1 oz) plain flour
- 3 Tbsp double cream

1 Preheat the oven to 150° C (300° F / gas 2). Trim the roots from the celery and any damaged outer stems. Cut off the leaves and reserve. Slice the celery in half lengthways and rinse well under cold running water. Shake off the excess water.

2 Bring a large, deep frying pan of water to the boil and cook the celery for 10 minutes. Carefully remove with a slotted spoon and place the celery in an oval or rectangular dish – this cooking water could be used for soups and stocks if liked. Sprinkle over the shallot or onion and carrots, and pour over the stock. Top with a few sprigs of thyme and season lightly. Cover tightly with foil and bake in the oven for about 45 minutes until tender.

3 Carefully remove the celery with a slotted spoon, reserving the cooking liquid, and place in a warm serving dish. Cover and keep warm. Strain the reserved cooking liquid into a saucepan. In a bowl, blend the butter and flour together and whisk small pieces into the stock, cooking over a low heat, until thickened. Cook for a further minute, stir in the cream and pour over the celery. Serve immediately sprinkled with the reserved celery leaves.

**FREEZING** Follow the recipe and strain the celery once it is cooked and place in a rigid container. Set aside to cool, allowing the cooking liquid to cool separately. When both are cold, pour the liquid over the celery, seal and freeze for up to six months. Defrost in the fridge overnight, reheat the celery in the stock until piping hot and continue with the recipe above.

# Buttered marrow with a crispy crust

Marrow has the reputation of being a bit on the bland side, but if you pep it up with fresh herbs it makes a good side dish and it's an ideal choice for feeding lots of people.

**Serves 6**

- 1 medium-size marrow (weighing approx. 900 g / 2 lb)
- 75 g (2½ oz) butter
- 2 Tbsp olive oil
- Salt and freshly ground black pepper
- 2 medium slices white bread
- 25 g (1 oz) unsalted cashews
- Small bunch fresh chives
- 1 shallot or small onion, peeled and finely chopped

1 Peel the marrow, cut in half lengthways and scoop out the seeds. Cut into 2.5 cm (1 in) chunks.

2 Melt 25 g (1 oz) butter with the olive oil in a large lidded frying pan until frothy. Add the marrow and plenty of seasoning and stir well for 2 minutes to coat in the butter and oil. Cover the pan and cook over a gentle heat for 7 to 8 minutes, stirring occasionally until just tender.

3 Meanwhile, tear the bread into pieces, then place in a blender or food processor with the cashews and chives. Blend for a few seconds until the mixture forms even crumbs. Melt the remaining butter in a frying pan until frothy and cook the shallot or onion for 4 to 5 minutes until softened but not browned. Stir in the breadcrumb mixture and cook for a further 2 to 3 minutes until well coated and evenly mixed.

4 Preheat the grill to a medium setting. Transfer the buttered marrow pieces with the cooking juices to a large ovenproof gratin dish. Sprinkle over the herby crumbs and cook under the grill for about 4 to 5 minutes until crisp and golden. Serve immediately as an accompaniment to roast or grilled meat.

**Variation:** You can use the same method for sliced courgettes, and also for squash or pumpkin but you will need to cook these longer in the butter to start with as they have a denser texture.

❄ **FREEZING** Not suitable

# Horseradish cream and onion gravy

No roast dinner is complete without horseradish sauce or gravy. For an extra rich gravy, replace 150 ml (5 fl oz) stock with the same amount of red wine. Here are two classic recipes.

**Serves 4**

**For the horseradish cream**

- 100 ml (3½ fl oz) double cream
- 45 g (1½ oz) piece horseradish root
- 1 tsp Dijon mustard
- 2 tsp white wine vinegar
- 1 tsp caster sugar
- Salt and freshly ground black pepper

**For the onion gravy**

- 2 Tbsp meat cooking juices and fat from the roasting pan or 25 g (1 oz) dripping or butter
- 2 medium onions, peeled and finely sliced
- 25 g (1 oz) plain flour
- 600 ml (1 pint) beef stock

1 Make the horseradish sauce just before serving. Lightly whip the double cream until just peaking. Peel and finely grate or mince the horseradish – see Cook's note below. Place in a small bowl, mix with the remaining ingredients and fold into the cream. Serve with hot or cold roast beef, cold ham, or smoked fish.

2 To make the gravy, reheat the pan juices in a saucepan or melt the dripping or butter, and gently fry the onions for about 15 minutes until very tender and lightly browned. Stir in the flour and cook for 1 minute. Remove from the heat and gradually blend in the stock. Return to the heat and bring to the boil, stirring, until thickened. Cook for a further minute before transferring to a warm gravy or sauce boat to serve. Serve hot to accompany sausages, roast beef, steak or roast chicken.

**COOK'S NOTE** Horseradish is very pungent when peeled and prepared, so handle with care. The easiest (and most comfortable) way to grate it is to use a food processor. It also discolours quickly.

**FREEZING** The horseradish cream is not suitable for freezing. For the gravy, allow to cool, then pack into a rigid container. Seal and freeze for up to three months. Defrost in the fridge overnight and reheat in a saucepan, stirring occasionally, until piping hot.

# Ratatouille   *See Page 112*

I've been making this tasty vegetable dish for years but until recently I used to make it quite chunky. After a friend made a much finer version for me, I've been cutting up the vegetables into small pieces and I much prefer it. It makes a great sauce and filling for pies and quiches, too.

**Serves 6**
- 1 large aubergine
- Salt
- 4 Tbsp olive oil
- 1½ tsp coriander seeds, lightly crushed
- 1 large onion, peeled and finely chopped
- 2 garlic cloves, peeled and finely chopped
- 1 red pepper, deseeded and finely chopped
- 1 green pepper, deseeded and finely chopped
- ½ small squash, peeled, seeds removed and finely diced
- 1 quantity of Fresh tomato sauce (see page 94)
- 1 bouquet garni (see page 55)
- 1 large courgette, trimmed and finely diced
- Freshly ground black pepper

**1** Trim the aubergine, cut into rounds about 1 cm (½ in) thick, then cut into small cubes. Layer in a colander or large sieve, sprinkling with salt as you go. Put the colander in a large bowl and set aside for 30 minutes. Rinse well and pat dry with kitchen paper.

**2** Meanwhile, heat the oil in a large saucepan and gently fry the coriander seeds, onion and garlic for about 5 minutes until softened but not browned. Stir in the chopped peppers and squash and stir well to coat in the onion mixture. Pour over the tomato sauce and add the bouquet garni. Bring to the boil, cover and simmer gently for 15 minutes.

**3** Stir in the courgette and aubergine, replace the lid and continue to cook for 20 to 25 minutes until tender and thick. Discard the bouquet garni and season with black pepper. Serve immediately as an accompaniment to grilled meat or fish, or toss into freshly cooked pasta as a sauce.

**COOK'S NOTE** If you haven't made a tomato sauce, then either use tinned chopped tomatoes or passata for convenience.

**FREEZING** Allow to cool, then ladle into rigid containers. Seal and freeze for up to six months. Defrost in the fridge overnight and reheat in a saucepan, adding a little more liquid if necessary, stirring occasionally, until piping hot.

# Parsnips with chorizo

We have a less spicy version of this dish with our Christmas dinner – simply replace the chorizo with smoked bacon and add a tablespoon of maple syrup or clear honey instead of the sugar. This is also good made with small waxy potatoes.

*Serves 4*

- 450 g (1 lb) parsnips
- 1 Tbsp sunflower oil
- 1 red onion, peeled and finely chopped
- 2 tsp caster sugar
- 115 g (4 oz) chorizo, skinned, if necessary, and chopped
- 2 Tbsp freshly chopped parsley

1 Peel the parsnips and cut into bite-size pieces about 2 cm (¾ in) thick. Bring a saucepan of lightly salted water to the boil and cook the parsnips for 4 minutes to half cook. Drain well and leave aside in a colander or sieve to dry.

2 Meanwhile, heat the oil in a frying pan and gently fry the onion for 5 minutes, to soften. Add the sugar and raise the heat, cook, stirring for 4 to 5 minutes until richly golden and caramelised. Set aside.

3 In a large frying pan, dry fry the chorizo until the juices and fat begin to run. Add the parsnips and onion mixture and stir well to coat in the cooking juices. Cover and cook over a low heat, stirring occasionally, for about 10 minutes until the parsnips are tender. Serve immediately, sprinkled with chopped parsley.

**FREEZING** Allow to cool then pack into a rigid container. Seal and freeze for up to three months. Defrost in the fridge overnight, turn into a frying pan and gently reheat, stirring, with a little water to prevent drying out, until piping hot.

# French-style peas with lettuce and glazed radishes *See Page 113*

A delicate flavoured dish and very attractive to look at. It is a real taste of the summer and a perfect accompaniment to fish or chicken dishes.

**Serves 4**

- 25 g (1 oz) unsalted butter
- 225 g (8 oz) small radishes, trimmed and washed
- 1 Tbsp raspberry vinegar (see page 80)
- 4 tsp caster sugar
- 675 g (1 lb 8 oz) fresh peas, shelled
- 2 small Little Gem or 1 heart sweet romaine or cos lettuce, trimmed and shredded
- Salt and freshly ground black pepper

1 Melt the butter in a small saucepan until bubbling, then add the radishes. Cook in the butter over a medium heat, stirring, for 5 minutes before adding the vinegar and 1 teaspoon of sugar. Stir well, cover and simmer gently for 3 to 4 minutes, shaking the pan occasionally, until the radishes are just tender and well coated in syrup. Remove from the heat and set aside.

2 Bring a saucepan of lightly salted water to the boil and add the peas and the remaining sugar. Cover and cook for about 10 minutes until just tender. Drain well and return to the saucepan. Stir in the radishes and juices, and add the shredded lettuce. Cook, stirring, for 2 minutes, to heat through and until the lettuce starts to wilt. Season to taste and serve immediately.

❄ **FREEZING** Not suitable

**COOK'S NOTE** Adding a little sugar to the cooking water helps keep the bright peas' green colour during cooking.

# Classic potato dauphinoise

A personal favourite which I always look out for on a menu. This melt-in-the-mouth potato dish is the perfect accompaniment to a roast such as lamb, chicken or pork.

*Serves 4*
- 1 garlic clove
- 75 g (2½ oz) lightly salted butter, softened
- 675 g (1 lb 8 oz) medium-size waxy potatoes such as Charlotte
- 150 ml (5 fl oz) milk
- 150 ml (5 fl oz) double cream
- ¼ tsp ground nutmeg
- Salt and freshly ground black pepper
- 2 Tbsp freshly chopped parsley

1 Preheat the oven to 160° C (325° F / gas 3). Peel and halve the garlic clove and rub the cut side around the inside of a 1.2 l (2 pint) gratin dish, then smear half the butter inside the dish.

2 Peel the potatoes and slice thinly – the thinner you cut them, the quicker the gratin will cook – then lay them neatly inside the prepared dish.

3 Mix the milk, cream and nutmeg together, and season well. Pour over the potatoes. Dot with the remaining butter. Stand the gratin dish on a baking sheet and bake in the oven for about 1½ hours or until very tender. Serve sprinkled with black pepper and chopped parsley.

**COOK'S NOTE** Try replacing some of the potato with sweet potato, parsnip, Jerusalem artichoke or celeriac.

**FREEZING** Allow to cool and either freeze whole, making sure the dish is freezer-proof, or divide into portions and pack into rigid containers. Wrap well in clear wrap and then foil, and freeze for up to six months. Defrost in the fridge overnight. Reheat in the oven at 180° C (350° F / gas 4), covered in foil, for 25 to 35 minutes depending on size, until piping hot.

# Potato and Jersusalem artichoke focaccia *See Page 114*

Homemade bread is tasty and impressive, and a lovely accompaniment to soups or dishes with lots of sauce or gravy.

**Serves 8**

- 450 g (1 lb) very strong white bread flour
- 1½ tsp salt
- 1½ tsp caster sugar
- 2½ tsp instant or fast-acting dried yeast
- 1 Tbsp finely chopped fresh rosemary
- 75 g (2½ oz) freshly grated Parmesan cheese
- 100 ml (3½ fl oz) good quality olive oil
- Approximately 200 ml (7 fl oz) lukewarm water
- Juice of 1 large lemon
- 225 g (8 oz) small waxy potatoes such as Charlotte, scrubbed
- 225 g (8 oz) Jerusalem artichokes
- Few sprigs fresh rosemary
- 1–2 tsp coarse sea salt

1 Sieve the flour, salt and sugar into a bowl and stir in the dried yeast, chopped rosemary and cheese. Make a well in the centre and add 75 ml (3 fl oz) oil and enough lukewarm water to form a firm mixture.

2 Turn the dough onto a lightly floured surface and knead for about 5 minutes to form a smooth, round ball. Place in a flour-dusted bowl, cover loosely with a tea towel or oiled clear wrap and stand in a warm place for about 1 hour until double the size.

3 Once the dough has risen, re-knead and press onto a greased baking sheet to form a 25 cm (10 in) round. Lightly cover with a piece of oiled clear wrap and leave in a warm place for about 1 hour until doubled in size. Preheat the oven to 200° C (400° F / gas 6).

4 Meanwhile, pour the lemon juice into a bowl and half fill with cold water. Thinly slice the potatoes and place in the lemony water. Peel the artichokes and slice very thinly, putting the slices in the lemony water to avoid discolouring. Bring a saucepan of water to the boil and blanch the vegetable slices for 1 minute only. Drain well and set aside to dry.

5 Brush the top of the dough with some of the remaining oil and arrange the sliced potatoes and artichokes neatly on top. Insert a few small sprigs of rosemary between the slices and sprinkle with coarse salt to taste. Drizzle with the remaining oil and bake in the middle of the oven for about 50 minutes to 1 hour, until crisp and golden and the vegetables are tender. Transfer to a wire rack to cool. Best served warm.

**FREEZING** Allow to cool and either leave whole or cut into wedges. Place on a tray lined with baking parchment and open freeze. Wrap well and keep for up to three months. Defrost at room temperature for 3 to 4 hours. Reheat on a baking tray in the oven at 200° C (400° F / gas 6) for about 15 minutes, brushing with more oil to prevent drying out, until piping hot.

# Runner beans with pears and bacon

Home-grown runner beans are probably my favourite of all vegetable produce, and this recipe is an excellent way to cook them. Serve with chicken, pork or chunky white fish.

*Serves 4*

- 450 g (1 lb) runner beans
- 2 small ripe pears
- 1 Tbsp lemon juice
- 175 g (6 oz) rindless unsmoked back bacon, trimmed and chopped
- 25 g (1 oz) butter
- Salt and freshly ground black pepper

1 Top and tail the runner beans and peel off any stringy edges, then slice thinly on the diagonal. Bring a saucepan of lightly salted water to the boil, add the beans, cover and cook for 5 to 7 minutes until just tender. Drain well.

2 Meanwhile, peel and core the pears. Cut into thin slices and sprinkle with lemon juice. Put the bacon in a frying pan and heat until the juices start to form. Add the butter and stir-fry for 5 minutes until golden and cooked through. Toss in the cooked beans and pear slices, and carefully mix together, stirring over a medium heat for about 2 minutes to heat through. Serve immediately seasoned with black pepper.

❄ **FREEZING** Not suitable

**COOK'S NOTE** This recipe works well with French beans and broad beans. Also try with peas, mange-tout and slices of courgette.

# Cherry tomato and sweet pepper upside-down tart  *See Page 115*

Tarte Tatin has now become a mainstream dessert, and this savoury version makes a good side dish or meal in its own right.

**Serves 6**

- 25 g (1 oz) unsalted butter
- 2 tsp caster sugar
- Salt and freshly ground black pepper
- Few sprigs fresh oregano
- Few sprigs fresh marjoram
- 1 small red pepper
- 300 g (10½ oz) cherry or small vine tomatoes, rinsed and stalks removed
- 250 g (9 oz) puff pastry, thawed if frozen
- 1–2 Tbsp balsamic vinegar

1 Preheat the oven to 200° C (400° F / gas 6). Lightly grease a 20 cm (8 in) round cake tin. Sprinkle the base with sugar and dot with the butter. Sprinkle with salt, black pepper and the herbs and set aside.

2 Remove the core from the pepper and slice into rings, cutting out any seeds that remain inside. Arrange over the base of the tin and fill the base with the cherry or vine tomatoes.

3 Roll out the pastry on a lightly floured surface to just larger than the size of the tin. Place on top of the tomatoes and tuck down the edges between the tin and the tomatoes. Place on a baking tray and bake for 30 to 35 minutes, until lightly golden and bubbling. Stand for 5 minutes and then turn out of the tin, taking care not to burn yourself on the juices. Serve immediately, pepper and tomato side up, drizzled with balsamic vinegar, and cut into wedges to accompany a light chicken or fish dish.

❋ **FREEZING**  Not suitable

**COOK'S NOTE**  For more of a main meal, cut into quarters, shave over pieces of Parmesan or pecorino cheese and serve with a dollop of fresh pesto sauce. You can use larger tomatoes for this recipe, just cut them in half and arrange in the bottom of the tin, uncut side down.

# DESSERTS AND PUDDINGS

## Blushing apples with strawberry rose ice cream   See Page 116

A very pretty pink dish of simple flavours and a real taste of summer. Pear halves or quarters poach just as well as the apples.

*Serves 6*

**For the ice cream**

- 350 g (12½ oz) strawberries, rinsed and hulled
- 115 g (4 oz) alpine strawberries or frais de bois, rinsed
- 2 Tbsp rose water (optional)
- 300 ml (½ pint) double cream
- Approximately 115 g (4 oz) icing sugar
- Juice of 1 lemon

**For the apples**

- 6 Tbsp caster sugar
- 6 eating apples
- 1 Tbsp lemon juice
- 150 ml (5 fl oz) sweet rosé wine

1 Start by making the ice cream. Put the strawberries in a blender or food processor with the rose water, if using, and blend for a few seconds until smooth. Whip the cream until just peaking and sieve in the icing sugar; fold into the cream along with the strawberry mixture and lemon juice. Taste and add more sugar if required.

2 Either churn in an ice cream maker or transfer to a freezer container, cover and place in the coldest part of the freezer for about 1½ to 2 hours until slushy, then beat well. Return to the freezer for a further hour before beating again. Repeat this process twice more, then freeze for at least 4 hours until firmly frozen. Stand at room temperature for about 15 minutes, to soften, before serving.

3 For the apples, pour 200 ml (7 fl oz) water in a saucepan and add the sugar. Heat gently, stirring until dissolved, then bring to the boil and simmer for 5 minutes.

4 Peel and core the apples, and cut into 1 cm (½ in) thick rings. Brush all over with lemon juice to prevent browning. Place in a saucepan and pour over the wine and hot syrup. Bring to the boil, cover and simmer gently for 5 minutes. Turn the apple rings over and cook for a further 5 minutes, until just tender. Remove from the heat and set aside to cool, then transfer to a serving bowl. Cover and chill for 2 hours. Serve with the ice cream.

**COOK'S NOTE** You can also make this ice cream with raspberry, blackberry, gooseberry or a fresh currant purée, adding more icing sugar if necessary.

**FREEZING** Ice cream only. Store sealed and labelled in the freezer for up to six months.

# Gooseberry and elderflower jelly

Adding elderflower to this gooseberry jelly mix gives it a flowery edge that I love. This light dessert is the perfect finish to a rich meal on a summer's evening.

**Serves 6**
- 450 g (1 lb) green gooseberries, topped and tailed
- 75–115 g (2½–4oz) caster sugar
- 15 g (½ oz) fresh elderflower heads or
- 2 Tbsp elderflower cordial (see Cook's note)
- Juice of ½ lemon
- 5 sheets of leaf gelatine
- 150 ml (5 fl oz) sweet dessert wine such as Muscat
- Pouring cream, to serve

1 Place the gooseberries in a saucepan with 75 g (2½ oz) sugar and elderflowers (do not add the cordial at this stage, if using). Add 2 tablespoons of water, bring to the boil, cover and simmer for 8 to 10 minutes until soft. Discard the elderflowers.

2 Transfer to a blender or food processor and blend until smooth. Push through a nylon sieve to make a smooth purée – approximately 450 ml (16 fl oz). Mix in the cordial, if using, and lemon juice. Taste and add more sugar if required. Set aside to cool.

3 Cut each leaf of gelatine into small pieces and place in a bowl. Spoon over 4 tablespoons of cold water and leave aside to soak for 10 minutes. Melt the gelatine over a pan of simmering water and set aside to cool.

4 Stir the dessert wine and gelatine into the gooseberry purée and pour into a 600 ml (1 pint) mould. Chill for at least 4 hours until set.

5 To serve, dip the mould in hot water for a few seconds to loosen, then invert onto a serving plate. Serve with pouring cream and decorate with fresh elderflowers if liked.

❋ **FREEZING** Not suitable

**COOK'S NOTE** If using fresh elderflower heads, rinse in running water and shake off excess. Trim away as much of the stalk as possible, leaving only the flower heads bunched together. If you have an elder tree, it is easy to make your own cordial: put 115 g (4 oz) rinsed elderflower heads in a saucepan with 500 ml (18 fl oz) water. Bring to the boil and simmer for 30 minutes. Strain through muslin and return the liquid to the saucepan. Stir in 350 g (12½ oz) caster sugar until dissolved, then bring to the boil and simmer for 15 minutes until syrupy and lightly golden. Pour into sterilised bottles, seal and cool. Store in the refrigerator and serve diluted. Makes approximately 600 ml (1 pint).

# Blueberry pie with lavender cream See Page 117

I had to include a classic pie in this section, and you can adapt the filling to use other favourite soft fruits as well as plums, peaches and greengages.

**Serves 6–8**

**For the pie**

- 350 g (12½ oz) plain flour
- ½ tsp salt
- 200 g (7 oz) unsalted butter
- 150 g (5½ oz) caster sugar
- 550 g (1 lb 3 oz) blueberries
- 4 tsp arrowroot
- 1 medium egg, beaten

**For the cream**

- 300 ml (½ pint) whipping cream
- 2 Tbsp icing sugar
- 1 tsp ground lavender buds (see page 52)

1 Preheat the oven to 200° C (400° F / gas 6). Sieve the flour and salt into a large bowl and rub in the butter. Stir in 4 tablespoons of caster sugar and bind together with approximately 4 tablespoons of cold water. Knead lightly to form a smooth dough. Wrap and chill for 30 minutes.

2 Roll out just over half the pastry on a lightly floured surface to fit a 20 cm (8 in) round pie dish or tin, 5 cm (2 in) deep. Cover and chill until required.

3 Meanwhile, prepare the filling. Leaving aside 300 g (10½ oz) blueberries, place the remaining in a saucepan with 3 tablespoons of water. Bring to the boil, cover and simmer for 3 to 4 minutes until very soft. Cool slightly, then push through a nylon sieve to make a purée. Return to the saucepan. Mix the arrowroot with 2 tablespoons of water to form a paste and add to the blueberry purée along with 3 tablespoons of the remaining caster sugar. Heat, stirring, bringing to the boil and cook until thickened. Remove from the heat and stir in the remaining blueberries. Set aside to cool.

4 Spoon the cooled filling into the pastry case. Roll out the remaining pastry to make a lid, then brush the edge of the case with beaten egg and seal the lid on top, pressing the edge all round with the prongs of a fork. Make two small slits in the middle of the lid, brush all over with egg and dredge with the remaining caster sugar. Place on a baking sheet. Bake for about 45 minutes until golden.

5 To make the lavender cream, whip the cream until just peaking. Sieve over the icing sugar and fold in, along with the lavender. Cover and chill until required. Serve the pie hot or cold with a dollop of lavender cream.

**FREEZING** Allow the pie to cool and freeze whole, making sure the dish is freezer-proof. Wrap well in clear wrap and then foil, and freeze for up to six months. Defrost in the fridge overnight and either serve cold, or reheat in the oven at 180° C (350° F / gas 4), covered in foil for 25 to 30 minutes until piping hot. Remove the foil for the last 5 minutes of cooking. The lavender cream is not suitable for freezing.

# Blackcurrant fool  *See Page 118*

An old-fashioned dessert that is an ideal way to use your favourite fruit. Homemade creamy custard and a simple fruit purée – nothing could be simpler or tastier.

**Serves 6**

- 450 g (1 lb) blackcurrants, stalks removed
- 7 Tbsp caster sugar
- 300 ml (½ pint) single cream
- 1 vanilla pod, split
- 4 medium egg yolks
- 100 ml (3½ fl oz) whipping cream

1 Put the blackcurrants in a saucepan with 4 tablespoons of water. Bring to the boil, cover and simmer for 6 to 7 minutes until juicy and very tender. Stir in 4 tablespoons of sugar to sweeten and set aside to cool.

2 Meanwhile, pour the cream into a separate saucepan and heat until hot but not boiling. Remove from the heat, add the vanilla pod and leave to infuse for 30 minutes. Discard the vanilla pod.

3 In a heatproof bowl, whisk the egg yolks with the remaining sugar until pale, thick and creamy. Pour over the vanilla-flavoured cream and whisk in gently to combine. Place on top of a saucepan of gently simmering water and cook stirring until thick enough to coat the back of a spoon – this will take 10 to 15 minutes. Remove from the saucepan, cover with a layer of buttered greaseproof paper and set aside to cool.

4 Once the blackcurrants have cooled, push them through a nylon sieve to make a purée. Whip the cream until just peaking and fold into the prepared custard along with the blackcurrant purée. Pile into six small tumblers or dessert glasses and chill for at least 1 hour before serving.

**COOK'S NOTE** Try this method with raspberries, redcurrants, gooseberries, blueberries or blackberries – adding the required amount of sugar to the stewed fruit to taste.

**FREEZING** Only the fruit purée can be frozen (see page 190).

# Oaty Scottish berry cream  *See Page 119*

Making the most of Scottish berries, this traditional dessert can be easily adapted using other fruits. Soft fruits such as strawberries, gooseberries or blueberries can be used instead if preferred.

*Serves 6*

- 350 g (12½ oz) blackberries, well rinsed and hulled
- 4–6 Tbsp heather honey
- 6 Tbsp fine oatmeal
- 450 ml (16 fl oz) double cream
- 6 Tbsp whisky
- 225 g (8 oz) loganberries, tayberries or raspberries, rinsed and hulled

**1** Place the blackberries in a blender or food processor with 4 tablespoons of honey and blend until puréed. Push through a nylon sieve to remove the seeds. Cover and chill until required.

**2** Sprinkle the oatmeal evenly over the bottom of a heavy-based frying pan and heat over a medium heat, stirring, for about 5 minutes until lightly toasted – take care not to burn the oatmeal. Allow to cool.

**3** When the oatmeal is cold, whip the cream until just peaking and fold in the whisky and oatmeal. Gently fold in the blackberry purée. Taste and add more honey if preferred. Divide the loganberries, tayberries or raspberries between six tumblers or serving glasses and pile the oaty blackberry cream on top. Cover and chill for at least 1 hour before serving.

**COOK'S NOTE** As an alternative to oatmeal, you could layer the berries in glasses with crunch oat cereal and the blackberry cream, omitting the whisky if preferred.

 **FREEZING** Only the berry purée can be frozen (see page 190).

# Trio of sorbets  *See Page 120*

One of the best ways to enjoy the flavours of summer by is making ice creams or sorbets. Here I am simply using the fruits by themselves, but I have suggested some additions in the note below if you want to add extra flavours.

**Serves 6**

- 525 g (1 lb 3 oz) caster sugar
- 350 g (12½ oz) fresh raspberries, rinsed and hulled
- 250 g (9 oz) fresh strawberries, rinsed and hulled
- 2 ripe medium-size peaches, skinned, stoned and chopped (see page 61)
- 6 Tbsp lemon juice

1 First make the sugar syrup. Place the sugar in a large saucepan and pour over 900 ml (1½ pints) cold water. Heat, stirring, until the sugar dissolves. Raise the heat, bring to the boil and simmer, without stirring, for 10 minutes. Remove from the heat and allow to cool completely.

2 Meanwhile, prepare the fruit purées. Blend each of the fruits separately in a blender or food processor until smooth, then rub each through a nylon sieve to remove seeds and membrane. Place each purée in a separate bowl, and cover and chill until required.

3 Divide the cold syrup between the three bowls. Add 2 tablespoons of lemon juice to each and mix well. Pour into separate small freezer-proof containers and freeze until just beginning to set round the edges, for about 1 to 1½ hours. Whisk well to break down the ice crystals evenly. Return to the freezer and freeze for a further 1½ to 2 hours, whisking every 30 minutes, until firm. Cover and store in the freezer until required.

4 To serve, stand the sorbets at room temperature for about 20 minutes until soft enough to scoop. Scoop one spoonful of sorbet in each serving glass and serve immediately.

**COOK'S NOTE** You can infuse the sugar syrup with various flavours to enhance the natural fruit. Here are my suggestions for each fruit:

**Raspberry:** rose water; orange blossom water; vodka; lime or orange zest.

**Strawberry:** rose water; white rum; vanilla; lavender; tarragon.

**Peach:** basil; rosemary; gin; almond; cinnamon.

 **FREEZING** Store sealed and labelled in the freezer for up to six months.

# Rhubarb and custard tarts  See Page 121

Another classic combination, but this time used in a very sophisticated way. As with other recipes in this section, you can top these tarts with any fresh or stewed fruit.

**Serves 6**

**For the custard**

- 1 medium egg yolk
- 25 g (1 oz) caster sugar
- 1 Tbsp plain flour
- 1 Tbsp cornflour
- 150 ml (5 fl oz) whole milk
- Few drops of vanilla extract

**For the pastry**

- Half quantity of pastry (see page 166)

**For the rhubarb**

- 350 g (12½ oz) thin stalks rhubarb
- 75 g (2½ oz) caster sugar
- 1 sheet fine leaf gelatine

1 Preheat the oven to 200° C (400° F / gas 6). To make the custard, whisk the egg yolk and sugar together until pale and thick. Whisk in the flour, cornflour and 2 tablespoons of milk to make a smooth paste. Heat the remaining milk until just below boiling point and pour over, whisking until smooth. Transfer to a saucepan and stir over a low heat until boiling, then cook for 2 minutes until thick. Remove from the heat, add a few drops of vanilla, cover the surface with buttered greaseproof paper and cool.

2 Divide the pastry into six equal portions and roll out each piece on a lightly floured surface to fit six 10 cm (4 in) loose-bottomed flan tins. Prick all over with a fork, arrange on a baking sheet and bake in the oven for about 15 minutes until lightly golden. Allow to cool then remove from the tins.

3 For the rhubarb, trim and cut into 7 cm (3 in) lengths. Place the sugar in a medium frying pan with a lid and pour in 100 ml (3½ fl oz) water. Heat gently, stirring until dissolved. Bring to the boil and simmer for 3 minutes.

4 Add the rhubarb, laying the pieces side by side. Bring to the boil, cover and simmer for about 5 minutes, carefully turning the rhubarb over halfway through, until just cooked. Remove from the heat and allow to cool. Remove the rhubarb pieces using a slotted spoon, reserving the juices, and place on a plate. Cover and chill until required. Strain the reserved juices into a jug and top up to 100 ml (3½ fl oz) with cold water if necessary.

6 Cut the gelatine into small pieces and place in a bowl. Spoon over 2 tablespoons of cold water and soak for 10 minutes. Melt the gelatine over a pan of simmering water and stir into the rhubarb syrup. Set aside to cool.

7 To assemble the tarts, spread some custard into each pastry case, leaving a small rim of pastry above the layer of custard. Arrange two to three pieces of rhubarb on top of each. Spoon over the prepared jelly to coat the fruit and flood the top of the custard. Chill for about 1 hour until set.

❄ **FREEZING**  Not suitable

# Sweet potato muffins

More a cake than a dessert, but I wanted to include some vegetable-based baking because the results give extra moistness to cakes. For a hearty pudding, these muffins are good served warm (un-iced) with maple syrup and custard or pouring cream.

*Makes 10*

- 225 g (8 oz) plain flour
- 1 tsp baking powder
- 1 tsp bicarbonate of soda
- ¼ tsp ground cardamom
- ¼ tsp salt
- 175 g (6 oz) caster sugar
- 45 g (1½ oz) unsweetened desiccated coconut
- 2 medium eggs, beaten
- 175 g (6 oz) unsalted butter, softened
- 100 ml (3½ fl oz) whole milk
- 250 g (9 oz) cooked smoothly mashed sweet potato
- 175 g (6 oz) icing sugar
- Few drops vanilla extract

1 Preheat the oven to 180° C (350° F / gas 4). Line 10 deep-cup muffin tins with paper muffin cases. Sift the flour, baking powder, bicarbonate of soda, cardamom and salt into a large mixing bowl. Stir in the sugar and coconut. Melt 75 g (2½ oz) of the butter and, in a separate bowl, mix into the eggs.

2 Make a well in the centre of the flour mix. Gradually blend in the eggs, melted butter and milk to form a thick batter. Fold in the sweet potato.

3 Divide between the muffin cases and bake in the oven for about 30 minutes until risen and lightly golden. Transfer to a wire rack to cool completely.

4 For the icing, beat the remaining butter until soft and gradually sieve and beat in the icing sugar, then add a few drops of vanilla extract to form a fluffy icing. Spread thickly over each muffin before serving.

**Variation:** Omit the coconut and cardamom, and replace the sweet potato with parsnip, 50 g (2 oz) caster sugar and an equal amount of heather honey. Infuse the milk with a small pinch of saffron and allow to cool before using. Cook and ice as above.

**COOK'S NOTE** The muffins are best wrapped and stored for 24 hours before icing and serving. This method works well for grated raw carrot or courgette, or cooked, smoothly mashed parsnip, floury potato, squash or pumpkin.

**FREEZING** Allow to cool completely, then place un-iced in a rigid freezer container. Seal well and freeze for up to three months. Thaw the muffins at room temperature. Make up frosting as above.

# Raspberry and redcurrant cheesecake  *See Page 122*

I love a good cheesecake, and this is one of my favourites, with just a hint of lemon and vanilla to flavour, and a deep and very fruity topping.

**Serves 8–10**

**For the cheesecake**

- 250 g (9 oz) shortbread fingers, finely crushed
- 75 g (2½ oz) unsalted butter, melted
- 600 g (1 lb 5 oz) full fat cream cheese
- 150 g (5½ oz) caster sugar
- 3 large eggs
- 3 large egg yolks
- ½ tsp finely grated lemon rind
- 1 tsp vanilla extract

**For the topping**

- 500 g (1 lb 2 oz) redcurrants, stalks removed
- 115 g (4 oz) caster sugar
- 3 Tbsp arrowroot
- 175 g (6 oz) raspberries, rinsed and hulled

- Pouring cream, to serve

1 Preheat the oven to 180° C (350° F / gas 4). Grease and line the base and sides of a 20 cm (8 in) round spring form cake tin. Wrap the outside of the tin in two layers of foil to make it water tight. Mix the biscuits with the butter and press into the base of the tin. Chill until required.

2 In a mixing bowl, beat the cream cheese, sugar, eggs, egg yolks, lemon rind and vanilla extract together until smooth. Pour over the base. Place the cheesecake in a roasting tin and pour boiling water to come halfway up the sides of the tin. Bake in the centre of the oven for about 1 hour until just set. Remove the tin carefully from the water, discard the foil and leave to cool in the tin on a wire rack for at least 1 hour for the top to firm up, before putting the fruit topping on.

3 Meanwhile, make the topping. Place the redcurrants in a saucepan with 6 tablespoons of water. Bring to the boil, cover and simmer for 4 to 5 minutes until very soft. Stir in the sugar. Cool slightly, then push through a nylon sieve to remove the seeds. Measure the quantity and make up to 500 ml (18 fl oz) with water if necessary. Set aside until the cheesecake is cooked.

4 When the cheesecake is ready, put the arrowroot in a saucepan and blend with a little of the fruit purée to make a paste. Stir in the remaining purée and gently bring to the boil, stirring, until thickened. Cool for 10 minutes. Arrange the raspberries on top of the cheesecake and spoon over the thickened purée to cover . Leave to cool completely, then chill for at least 2 hours. To serve, remove from the tin and accompany with pouring cream.

✳ **FREEZING**  Not suitable

**COOK'S NOTE** This fruit topping can be easily adapted using other fruits, such as blackcurrants, blackberries, blueberries or gooseberries – simply adjust the sugar quantity in the topping to taste.

# Damson flummery

It was the name of this dessert that first attracted me to it, and it turned out to be yet another way of using one fruit to its best advantage with just a few key ingredients. Also good made with plums, greengages or peaches.

### Serves 6

- 450 g (1 lb) damsons, stalks removed
- 115 g (4 oz) light brown sugar
- 1 small cinnamon stick, broken
- 5 Tbsp ruby port
- 2 sheets fine leaf gelatine
- 300 ml (½ pint) double cream

1 Place the damsons in a saucepan with the sugar, cinnamon and port. Cover and cook over a low heat for about 10 minutes until the damsons are very soft. Cool for 10 minutes, discard the cinnamon stick, then push through a nylon sieve to make a purée. Set aside to cool completely.

2 Cut the gelatine into small pieces and place in a bowl. Spoon over 2 tablespoons of cold water and leave aside to soak for 10 minutes. Melt the gelatine over a pan of simmering water and set aside to cool.

3 Whip the cream until just peaking. Pour the gelatine into the damson purée and mix well. Lightly fold the whipped cream into the damson mixture to give a rippled effect, then pile into six serving glasses. Cover and chill for at least 1 hour before serving.

❄ **FREEZING** Not suitable

**COOK'S NOTE** Damsons have an intense flavour when cooked on their own; if you prefer, cook them with plums or cooking apples to temper their richness.

# PRESERVES

## Marinated artichoke hearts with herbs and garlic *See Page 123*

Although there's quite a bit of preparation involved before you cook a globe artichoke, the effort is worthwhile. Here I'm preserving the hearts in oil, but you can eat them as a vegetable as soon as they are cooked – hot or cold.

*Serves 4*

- 2 lemons
- 6 prepared globe artichoke hearts (see page 15)
- 6 garlic cloves, peeled and halved
- 4 bay leaves
- 4 sprigs rosemary
- 4 sprigs thyme
- 250 ml (9 fl oz) dry white wine
- Approximately 250 ml (9 fl oz) good quality light olive oil

1 Cut the lemons in half and squeeze the juice of three halves into a bowl. Fill the bowl with cold water and add the squeezed lemon halves. Cut the artichoke hearts into quarters and immediately plunge in the lemony water to prevent blackening. Pull out any remaining choke from each piece if necessary.

2 Place half the garlic and 2 sprigs each of herbs in a saucepan. Pour over the wine and squeeze in the remaining lemon juice. Add the artichoke hearts, bring to the boil, and cover and simmer for 10 to 15 minutes until just tender. Remove from the heat and allow to cool, turning occasionally. Cover and chill for at least 2 hours or overnight, turning occasionally.

3 The next day, drain the artichoke hearts, pat dry with absorbent paper, then arrange on a wire rack and allow to air dry for 20 minutes.

4 Pour 1 cm (½ in) depth of olive oil into a cold 500 ml (18 fl oz) sterilised preserving jar (see page 189) and pack the artichoke hearts with the reserved herbs and garlic, pouring in the oil and swivelling the jar to remove any air bubbles as you go, until full. Top up with oil and seal. Label and store in a cool, dark, dry place for at least one month before serving. Will keep for six months.

# Baby aubergines in spiced oil  *See Page 124*

If you have larger varieties of aubergine, simply slice into rounds or quarters and proceed with the recipe below.

**Serves 6**

• 8 baby aubergines
• Salt
• Approximately 250 ml (9 fl oz) good quality light olive oil
• 1 bay leaf
• 1 red chilli, halved and deseeded
• 1 tsp coriander seeds, toasted and lightly crushed
• 1 tsp black peppercorns, lightly crushed

1 Trim the aubergines, and cut into lengthways slices about 1 cm (½ in) thick. Layer in a glass colander or sieve, sprinkling with plenty of salt, and cover the top of the slices with baking parchment. Stand in a large mixing bowl and place a weighted plate on top. Leave in a cool place overnight.

2 The next day, rinse the aubergines well. Arrange on a clean tea towel or absorbent kitchen paper and allow to air dry.

3 Transfer the aubergines to a shallow dish and drizzle with 4 tablespoons of oil, stirring well to coat. Heat a large griddle pan until very hot – it is ready when you can no longer hold a flat hand 2.5 cm (1 in) away from the hot surface for 10 seconds. Cook the slices in batches, pressing them into the pan (I use the flat head of a potato masher to do this) for 2 to 3 minutes on each side, until tender and scorched. Spread out on a wire rack to cool.

4 Pour 1 cm (½ in) depth of olive oil into a 500 ml (18 fl oz) sterilised preserving jar (see page 189) and pack the aubergines with the bay leaf, chilli and spices, pouring in the oil and swivelling the jar to remove any air bubbles as you go, until full. Top up with oil and seal. Label and store in a cool, dark, dry place for at least one month before serving. Will keep for six months.

**COOK'S NOTE** Baby peppers can be preserved in the same way. Pierce whole all over with a fork and place in a colander in a bowl. Sprinkle with salt and leave overnight. Rinse well, pat dry and leave to drain on wads of kitchen paper. Roast on a rack at 200° C (400° F / gas 6) for about 25 minutes until soft and lightly browned. Cool for 10 minutes, then carefully pull out the stalk and as many seeds as you can. Leave to drain on a wire rack and then on wads of kitchen paper until cool. Pack into a sterilised jar as above with olive oil.

# Slow roast preserved tomatoes with herbs

Succulent and vibrant, these tender tomatoes are the perfect reminder of summer when there's an autumnal nip in the air.

**Serves 12**

- 1.8 kg (4 lb) well flavoured, ripe plum or other fleshy tomatoes
- Salt
- Small bunch fresh marjoram
- Small bunch fresh oregano
- Approximately 500 ml (18 fl oz) good quality extra virgin olive oil

1 Preheat the oven to its lowest setting – ideally about 60° C (140° F). It should not exceed 80° C (175° F). Line two large baking sheets with foil and place wire racks to fit on top.

2 Cut the tomatoes in half and scoop out the seeds using a teaspoon. Place cut-side down on wads of absorbent kitchen paper whilst preparing each tomato. Sprinkle the cut side with salt and place cut-side down on the prepared wire racks and trays. Place in the oven, leaving the door slightly ajar if necessary to ensure the tomatoes dry rather than cook, and leave for about 8 hours, turning over after 6 hours, until dry to the touch but still fleshy and not papery. Remove from the oven and allow to cool.

3 Pour 1 cm (½ in) depth of olive oil into a cold 700 ml (25 fl oz) sterilised preserving jar (see page 189). Pack the tomatoes and herbs in the jar, and pouring in the oil as you go, swivel the jar to remove any air bubbles. Top up with oil and seal. Label and store in a cool, dark, dry place for at least one month before serving. Will keep for six months.

**COOK'S NOTE** If you can't wait to eat some, drizzle a few with olive oil and sprinkle over some slivers of sliced garlic. Place in the oven at about 150° C (300° F / gas 2) for about 10 minutes to warm through. Season with black pepper and serve warm with fresh basil.

# Wild strawberry jam

I have loads of wild strawberries growing in my garden and although it takes a long time to pick enough for jam making, when mixed with the larger variety, you are still able to achieve an interestingly perfumed jam. I like to add rosewater to emphasise the taste.

*Makes approximately*
*900 g (2 lb)*

- 450 g (1 lb) strawberries, rinsed and hulled
- 175 g (6 oz) wild or alpine strawberries, rinsed
- 450 g (1 lb) granulated sugar
- 2 Tbsp lemon juice
- 1 Tbsp rosewater (optional)

1 If the strawberries are very large, cut them into small pieces. Place in a preserving pan or large saucepan and add half the wild strawberries. Heat until hot and simmering, then add the sugar and lemon juice. Stir over a low heat until the sugar dissolves.

2 Raise the heat and boil rapidly until the setting point is reached (see page 189) and stir in the remaining wild strawberries and rosewater, if using. Spoon into hot jars and seal as described on page 189.

**Variation:** For all strawberry jam, use 900 g (2 lb) fruit to 800 g (1 lb 12 oz) sugar and 4 tablespoons of lemon juice.

**COOK'S NOTE** When using frozen fruit for jam making, you will need to double the amount of lemon juice used, otherwise the jam will not set very well.

# Marrow, ginger and orange conserve

Not an obvious choice for jam making, but marrows are a traditionally preserved vegetable from yesteryear, and the result is an earthier version of a melon jam.

*Makes approximately*
*700 g (1 lb 9 oz)*

• 450 g (1 lb) peeled and
  seeded marrow flesh
  (weighing about 900 g /
  2 lb) or 1 medium
  marrow
• 25 g (1. oz) preserved
  ginger in syrup, finely
  chopped
• 1 Tbsp ginger syrup
• Finely grated rind and
  juice of 1 large orange
• 450 g (1 lb) granulated
  sugar
• 2 Tbsp lemon juice

1 Cut the marrow into 1 cm (½ in) thick pieces. Place in a large glass bowl and stir in the chopped ginger, ginger syrup and orange rind. Stir well, cover and stand for 2 hours to allow the flavours to develop.

2 Transfer to a preserving pan or large saucepan, add the orange and lemon juices and stir over a low heat until the sugar dissolves. Raise the heat and boil steadily for about 15 minutes, until syrupy and the setting point is reached (see page 189). Allow to cool for 15 minutes, stir to distribute the fruit pieces, then spoon into hot jars and seal as described on page 189.

**COOK'S NOTE** Other citrus fruits such as lemons or limes can be used instead of oranges. For melon jam, use the same quantity of green melon as marrow, but add 4 tablespoons of lemon juice instead of orange.

# Redcurrant and mint jelly  *See Page 125*

I always had mint sauce with our roast lamb as a child, although now I prefer redcurrant jelly. This preserve means you can have two traditional accompaniments in one hit. Omit the mint and vinegar for a straight fruit jelly.

*Makes approximately*
*900 g (2 lb)*
- 900 g (2 lb) firm
  redcurrants, rinsed
- Approximately 450 g
  (1 lb) granulated sugar
  per 600 ml (1 pint)
  juice
- 2 Tbsp white malt
  vinegar
- 2–3 Tbsp freshly
  chopped mint

1 Place the redcurrants in a preserving pan or large saucepan and pour over 150 ml (5 fl oz) water. Bring to the boil and simmer for 5 to 10 minutes until very tender, crushing them whilst they cook.

2 Strain the fruit and its juices through a jelly bag or some clean muslin suspended over a clean bowl – it will take about 6 hours to allow the fruit left behind to become dry – don't be tempted to squeeze the mixture.

3 Discard the fruit in the muslin. Measure the juice and pour back into the saucepan. Add 450 g (1 lb) sugar per 600 ml (1 pint) juice. Stir in the vinegar and mint. Heat, stirring over a low heat until the sugar is dissolved. Raise the heat and boil rapidly for about 15 minutes until the setting point is reached (see page 189). Skim off any surface foam using a flat spoon. Pour into hot jars and seal as described on page 189.

**COOK'S NOTE** If the redcurrants are very ripe, you will not need to add any water to the mixture at the beginning. Blackcurrants also make an excellent jelly and are especially good flavoured with mint.

# Sweet pepper and chilli jam

Chilli heat is entirely down to personal taste so I've created a chutney-like jam that's not too hot but has bit of a kick. Add a couple more chillies and another teaspoon of hot smoked paprika if you want more heat.

*Makes 1 kg (2 lb 3 oz)*

- 450 g (1 lb) sweet red peppers (weight when cored and deseeded) or 3 large peppers
- 2 large fleshy red chillies, halved and deseeded
- 225 g (8 oz) red onions, peeled
- 350 g (12½ oz) cooking apples (weight when peeled and cored) or 3 medium apples
- 225 ml (8 fl oz) cider vinegar
- 175 g (6 oz) granulated sugar
- 1 tsp salt
- ½ tsp freshly ground black pepper
- 1 tsp hot smoked paprika

1 Cut the peppers and chillies into small pieces, and finely chop the onions and apples. Place in a preserving pan or large saucepan and pour over the vinegar. Bring to the boil, partially cover and simmer for 20 minutes, stirring occasionally and mashing down with a wooden spoon until tender. Remove from the heat and cool for 10 minutes.

2 Either transfer the mixture to a blender or food processor or using a hand blender, blend the pepper mixture until smooth and thick. Return to the saucepan if necessary and stir in the sugar, salt and black pepper. Cook, stirring, over a low heat until dissolved, then cook steadily, uncovered, for 20 minutes, stirring occasionally, until the mixture looks like a thick jam. Stir in paprika to taste, then spoon into hot jars and seal (see page 189).

**COOK'S NOTE** This chutney goes well with cheeses, smoked meats, sausages and barbecued food. You can also add 2 cloves chopped garlic with the onions for extra flavour.

# Spiced plum chutney

A lovely fruity accompaniment ideal served at Christmas with cold meats, pâtés or cheeses. You could use peaches instead of plums if you have them.

**Makes 2.7 kg
(6 lb 2 oz)**

- 900 g (2 lb) cooking plums
- 450 g (1 lb) cooking apples
- 450 g (1 lb) onions, peeled
- 2 garlic cloves, peeled
- 5 cm (2 in) piece root ginger, peeled
- 600 ml (1 pint) white malt vinegar
- 1 cinnamon stick, broken
- 2 tsp mustard seeds, toasted and lightly crushed
- 2 tsp garam masala
- 2 bay leaves
- 450 g (1 lb) light brown sugar
- 225 g (8 oz) sultanas
- 1–2 tsp salt

1 Roughly chop the plums and place in a preserving pan or large saucepan. Finely chop the apples, onions, garlic and ginger. Pour over the vinegar and add the spices and bay leaves. Bring to the boil and simmer for 10 to 15 minutes, stirring occasionally, until tender.

2 Stir in the sugar and sultanas, and stir over a low heat until dissolved, then cook steadily for 35 to 40 minutes, stirring occasionally, until the mixture looks like thick jam. Discard the bay leaves and cinnamon. Stir in salt to taste, then spoon into hot jars and seal (see page 189).

**COOK'S NOTE** For a speedier flavouring, replace the spices with 1 tablespoon of mild curry powder.

# Sweet piccalilli  *See Page 126*

When I was a little girl, we had an elderly neighbour who used to give me tiny jars of homemade preserves, and her sweet piccalilli is one that has stuck in my mind as being particularly memorable. Here is my version.

*Makes approximately*
*1.35 kg (3 lb)*
- 900 g (2 lb) prepared mixed vegetables – traditionally cauliflower, green beans, marrow, courgette, onion and cucumber
- 1.2 l (40 fl oz) wet brine (see Cook's note)
- 600 ml (1 pint) spiced vinegar for vegetables (see Cook's note)
- 50 g (2 oz) plain flour
- 1 Tbsp mustard powder
- 2 tsp ground turmeric
- 50 g (2 oz) caster sugar

1 Cut the vegetables into small pieces no bigger than 1 cm (½ in) in size. Place in a large glass bowl and pour over the wet brine. Cover loosely and stand in a cool place for 24 hours to soak.

2 The next day, in a large saucepan, blend 4 tablespoons of the vinegar with the flour, mustard powder and turmeric to form a paste. Gradually blend in the remaining vinegar and add the sugar to make a sauce. Slowly bring to the boil, stirring, and cook for 1 minute to thicken. Drain the vegetables well but do not rinse them, and stir them in the mustard sauce, making sure they are well covered. Bring to the boil and cook for 1 minute – this will ensure the vegetables still have 'bite' when the pickle is eaten. Longer cooking will result in a softer pickle. Stir gently, then spoon into hot sterilised jars and seal (see page 189).

**COOK'S NOTE**

**For the wet brine:** Dissolve 50 g (2 oz) salt to 600 ml (1 pint) water in a glass bowl or container.

**For basic spiced vinegar for vegetables:** Mix 2 tablespoons each of mustard seeds, black peppercorns and allspice berries with 1 tablespoon of cloves, a small piece of root ginger, grated, and 10 small dried chillies, then tie in a small square of clean muslin. Add to a saucepan containing 600 ml (1 pint) malt vinegar. Bring to the boil and simmer for 10 to 15 minutes depending on how strong you want the spice flavour to be. Allow to cool, then discard the spice bag. Bottle and store until required.

# Pickled red cabbage with onion and beetroot

No Boxing Day buffet table is complete without pickled red cabbage. The crisp texture is perfect for the cold leftovers and jacket potatoes – roll on Christmas!

**Makes 1.8 kg (4 lb)**
- 1 medium red cabbage
- Salt
- 4 medium red onions
- 600 ml (1 pint) wet brine (see page 182)
- 350 g (12½ oz) cooked, peeled beetroot
- 600 ml (1 pint) spiced vinegar for vegetables (see page 182)

1 Trim away the outside leaves from the cabbage. Using a stainless steel knife, cut the cabbage into fine shreds across the grain. Slice out any of the tough stalks.

2 Place a layer of cabbage in a glass bowl and sprinkle generously with salt. Continue filling the bowl ending with a layer of salt. Cover loosely with a clean tea towel and stand in a cool place for 24 hours. Rinse well in cold water, then shake off any excess water.

3 Meanwhile, peel and shred the onions. Place in a glass bowl and pour over the wet brine. Cover loosely with a clean tea towel and stand in a cool place for 24 hours. Drain well without rinsing.

4 The next day, either slice or dice the beetroot depending on preference. Pack layers of cabbage, onion and beetroot in cold large sterilised jars (see page 189) and completely cover with vinegar, then seal down. Allow to mature for two weeks before using. Store for up to three months as cabbage may become soft after this time.

**Variations**

**For cucumbers:** Wipe the cucumber without peeling. If small leave whole but pierce all over with a fork, otherwise cut into neat even-size pieces. Layer with salt as above and leave for 24 hours. Rinse well, then pack into cold, large sterilised jars, adding sprigs of dill and celery leaves with the cucumbers. Cover with spiced vinegar and seal (see page 189).

**Courgettes** and **marrow** can be pickled using the same method. Marrow should be peeled, seeded and diced, whilst courgettes only need slicing, or piercing if baby variety.

For **small onions** and **shallots**, peel and soak in wet brine for 24 hours. Drain and rinse well, then pack in vinegar as above. Add 1 tablespoon of caster sugar to the vinegar for a sweeter pickle.

# Blackcurrant cordial  *See Page 127*

This refreshing drink packs a real punch with its intense curranty flavour. Pour over ice and dilute with chilled spring water to taste.

**Makes approximately 700 ml (25 fl oz)**

- 900 g (2 lb) blackcurrants, rinsed
- Approximately 300 g (10½ oz) caster sugar per 500 ml (18 fl oz) juice
- Juice of 1 lime

1 Place the blackcurrants in a preserving pan or large saucepan and pour over 600 ml (1 pint) water. Bring to the boil and simmer for 5 to 7 minutes, crushing them whilst they cook, until very tender and soft.

2 Strain the fruit and its juices through a jelly bag or some clean muslin suspended over a clean bowl – it will take at least 8 hours to allow the fruit left behind to stop dripping and drain thoroughly – don't be tempted to squeeze the mixture.

3 Discard the fruit in the muslin. Measure the juice and pour back into the saucepan. Add 300 g (10½ oz) sugar per 500 ml (18 fl oz) juice. Heat gently, stirring over a low heat just until the sugar dissolves but do not boil. Remove from the heat and stir in the lime juice. Pour into hot sterilised bottles (see page 189) and seal. Store in the fridge for up to three months.

**COOK'S NOTE** For a refreshing drink, rinse a few sprigs of mint and shake off excess water. Pack into a tall tumbler and bruise lightly with a spoon. Add a few cubes of ice and spoon over 2 tablespoons of blackcurrant cordial . Top up with sparkling or soda water.

# Spiced pears  *See Page 128*

Another old fashioned method for preserving fruit that gives it an interesting flavour. I like to use spiced fruits in a trifle with a big slug of sherry or brandy.

*Makes 1.35 kg (3 lb)*
- 900 g (2 lb) firm dessert pears
- Pared rind of 1 lemon
- 600 ml (1 pint) basic spiced vinegar for fruit (see Cook's note)
- 600 g (1 lb 5 oz) granulated sugar

1 If the pears are small, simply peel them and remove as much of the core as possible, but leave whole. Otherwise, peel, core and halve or quarter them. Place in a large saucepan with the lemon rind and pour over the vinegar. Bring to the boil and simmer for 5 to 10 minutes until just tender.

2 Lift the pears from the pan with a slotted spoon and pack into hot sterilised jars (see page 189). Stir the sugar into the vinegar until dissolved then bring to the boil and cook for about 10 minutes until syrupy. Pour over the pears until completely covered and seal.

## Variations

**Apples:** Using tart dessert apples or small cooking apples, prepare as for pears and cook until just tender, omitting the lemon rind and adding extra cinnamon if liked. Proceed as above.

**Quince:** Use peeled, halved or quartered and cored quince and cook as for pears. Quince make a particularly delicious preserve.

Small fruit such as **blackberries, gooseberries, damsons** and **plums** can all be successfully spiced and preserved in this way. Choose firm fruit and cook lightly. You can adjust the spice mix and strength in accordance to what you are preserving.

### COOK'S NOTE

**For basic spiced vinegar for fruit:** Tie a small cinnamon stick, broken in half in a small square of clean muslin with 10 cloves, 1 teaspoon of allspice berries and a piece of blade mace (optional). Add to a saucepan containing 600 ml (1 pint) cider or white malt vinegar. Bring to the boil and simmer for 10 to 15 minutes depending on how strong you want the spice flavour to be. Allow to cool, then discard the spice bag. Bottle and store until required.

# Rumtopf

This is a recipe that can't be rushed. The aim is to keep adding to the mixture as each fruit comes into season, and by winter, you'll have an extremely delicious and heady concoction that will help keep the winter blues at bay!

**Makes:** This depends on how much fruit you add to the basic mix. The basic mix will serve approximately 10 people.

**To start the rumtopf**
- 900 g (2 lb) suitable assorted fruit (see Cook's note)
- 300 g (10½ oz) caster sugar
- 1 litre (35 fl oz) strong dark rum, light rum or brandy

**To add to the rumtopf**
- Seasonal fruits in the proportion of 450 g (1 lb) for every 150 g (5½ oz) caster sugar
- Extra dark rum, light rum or brandy, as required

1 Place the rinsed and prepared fruit in a large bowl layering with sugar as you go. Cover loosely with a clean tea towel and stand in a cool place overnight.

2 Carefully mix in the rum and ladle into a special ceramic rumtopf jar or a tall, glass preserving jar. Make sure the fruits are well submerged in the rum by covering the top with a scrunched up piece of greaseproof paper and a saucer to weigh the fruits down. If using a rumtopf jar, cover the top with cling film, then place the lid on top – this will help prevent loss of flavour and aroma. If using a preserving jar, seal the top as per design. Store in a cool dark place or the bottom of the fridge.

3 As time progresses, add more fruit and sugar in the proportions given above, stirring the contents gently to mix. Each time replace with a clean piece of greaseproof paper and the lid. After a month, you may want to add more rum depending on how strong you want the finished result to be.

4 If you start in June, with the strawberry season, and add each fruit as in comes into season, the mix will be ready by Christmas. It is ideally served with cream or ice cream. It also makes a good base for a trifle.

**COOK'S NOTE** Suitable fruits for a rumtopf are strawberries, cherries, raspberries, tayberries, loganberries, blackberries, gooseberries, red, white and blackcurrants, blueberries, plums, pears, peaches, melon and pineapple. All fruit should be in perfect condition, well rinsed and dried, and prepared as for eating in a fruit salad.

# Dried apple rings

You can re-hydrate these fruits by cooking in a compote with other dried fruit. They make a lovely sweet snack and are great dippers for a creamy blue cheese dip.

*Makes about 100 g*
*(3½ oz) rings*
• Juice of I lemon
• 4 firm, ripe, blemish-free
   eating apples

1 Preheat the oven to its lowest setting – ideally at 60° C (140° F). It should not exceed 80° C (175° F). Line 2 large baking sheets with foil and place wire racks to fit on top.

2 Pour the lemon juice in a bowl and add 600 ml (I pint) cold water. Rinse and pat dry the apples and carefully push out the core. Slice the apples very thinly – about 3 mm (⅛ in) thick – and place in the lemon water to prevent discolouration.

3 Drain the apple rings and pat dry with absorbent kitchen paper. Arrange on the wire racks and place in the oven, leaving the door slightly ajar if necessary to ensure the apple rings dry rather than cook, and leave for about 4 hours depending on the temperature of the oven, turning after 2 hours, until the apple rings are dry and leathery. Allow to cool before packing in between layers of baking parchment in airtight containers. Store in a cool place but not in the fridge as this will soften them.

**Variations:**
**For thicker apple rings:** Cut to a thickness of 6 mm (¼ in). These will take 6 to 8 hours, turning after 3 hours.
**Peaches and nectarines:** Peel halved and stoned fruits take 36 to 48 hours to dry out. Cut into slices, they will take 12 to 16 hours.
**Pears:** Choose small firm fruit. Peel, core and cut in lengthways slices or in half, and place in lemon juice as above. Pear slices will dry as for apples, but pear halves will take between 36 and 48 hours to dry out.
**Plums:** Choose firm, unblemished fruit. Rinse and pat dry, then cut in half and remove the stone. Plums will take 18 to 24 hours to dry depending on size.
**Berries:** Choose firm fruit in perfect condition. Hull or remove stalks, rinse and pat dry. Leave whole and dry for 12 to 18 hours.

# Rhubarb leather

An old fashioned sweetie that makes a stunning decoration if fashioned into shape. Fill cones of leather with cream and fruit purée. Savoury leathers make unusual canapés filled with cream cheese, mayonnaise, pesto sauce or bundles of vegetables.

*Makes approximately*
*20 squares*

• Few drops sunflower oil
• 450 g (1 lb) rhubarb
• 250 g (9 oz) + 3 Tbsp caster sugar
• Few drops pink food colouring (optional)

1 Preheat the oven to its lowest setting – ideally at 60° C (140° F). It should not exceed 80° C (175° F). Line a large baking sheet with foil and grease very lightly with sunflower oil. Rinse and trim the rhubarb, then slice thinly. Place in a large saucepan, cover and heat gently until the rhubarb starts to steam and the juices begin to run. Stir in 250 g (9 oz) of the sugar and continue to cook gently, stirring, until the sugar dissolves, then raise the heat slightly and cook for 25 to 35 minutes, stirring occasionally, until very tender, thick and pulpy – the time taken will depend on how juicy the rhubarb is. Cool slightly, then push through a nylon sieve to form a smooth thick purée. Depending on the variety of rhubarb used, if you want to leave the rhubarb a natural colour, then omit the food colouring, otherwise add a few drops to achieve your desired colour.

2 Using a palette knife, spread the purée across the prepared baking sheet to a thickness of 3 mm (⅛ in), tapping the baking sheet on the work surface to smooth the purée. Place the tray in the oven, leaving the door slightly ajar if necessary to ensure the leather dries rather than cooks, and leave for 6 to 8 hours depending on the temperature of the oven, until the leather is firm but still pliable – it should not be sticky at all. Sprinkle with half the remaining caster sugar and allow to cool.

3 Cut into neat 9 cm (3½ in) squares and carefully peel away the foil. Dust the peeled side with the last of the sugar. The squares can be stored flat in between layers of baking parchment in airtight containers, or rolled tightly in tubes, or formed into cones. Will keep for about one month.

**Variations:** Other successful fruits to use include strawberries, raspberries, blackberries and pears. If the fruit is sweeter, then simply reduce the sugar to taste. **Note:** Sieving will remove the seeds from berries.

Sweet vegetables like **carrots**, **tomatoes** and **squash** make interesting vegetable leathers: just add a small amount of sugar to taste.

# PRESERVATION TECHNIQUES

## Jam and chutney making

### CHOOSING AND PREPARATION

It is essential that you start with the best quality produce in order to prevent rapid deterioration during storage. Fruit and vegetables should be slightly underripe or perfectly ripe depending on the recipe; blemish-free, and especially free from mould and mildew. They should be correctly prepared.

### COOKING FRUIT

Prepared fruit is often simmered either on its own or with liquid before sugar is added. Cook the fruit slowly, without covering (unless otherwise stated), stirring occasionally until just softened. This will allow you to obtain the maximum amount of juice from the fruit. If there is a lack of juice, add a bit more water – this might occur if the fruit is firmer than usual. Take care not to overcook the fruit at this stage otherwise flavour and colour will be impaired.

### TESTING FOR SETTING POINT FOR JAMS, JELLIES, MARMALADE, CONSERVES AND FRUIT CHEESE

There are 2 main ways that I use to find out if a preserve has reached the right point in order to set:

- **Using a sugar thermometer** For jam, marmalade, conserves and fruit cheese, an acceptable reading range is from 104°–105.5° C (219°–222° F). The lower temperature will give a softer set than the higher one – used for conserves. Use the higher temperature for fruit cheeses. For jellies, use 104°–105° C (219°–221° F).
- **The wrinkle test** Take the saucepan of boiling preserve off the heat and quickly spoon a little preserve on to a cold flat plate; allow to cool. If the preserve is ready, a slight skin will form on the spoonful and will wrinkle when pushed with your finger. Return the saucepan to the boil if the preserve isn't ready and retest in about 2 minutes.

### PREPARING STORAGE JARS AND BOTTLES

Use sound glass containers and bottles with no chips or cracks. Wash thoroughly in very hot water with mild detergent, and rinse well. To sterilise jars and bottles, put them open side up in a deep saucepan, cover with boiling water and boil for 10 minutes. Carefully lift out with tongs and leave to drain upside down on a thick clean towel. Dry with a clean cloth if necessary and place on a baking tray lined with a few layers of kitchen paper; keep warm in the oven on the lowest setting until ready to fill.

### FILLING THE JARS

A clean ladle or small heatproof jug will be useful to help you transfer the preserve to the prepared jar or bottle. If the preserve is very fruity or contains rind and small pieces, stir well before putting in the jars. Fill to within 6 mm (¼ in) of the top of the jar. Half filled jars of preserve should be cooled, sealed and kept in the fridge and eaten as soon as possible.

### SEALING

To prevent spoiling during storage it is essential to achieve an air tight seal on your preserves. As soon as the preserve is in the jars, place a waxed paper circle directly on the top of the jam – available in packs of jam pot covers. Either top with a screw-on lid or seal tightly with the transparent jam pot covers and an elastic band. If you have lots of jars to fill, it is better to allow the preserve to cool completely in the jars before sealing with waxed paper circles and lids. Avoid covering semi-cold preserves as too much condensation will form and this could encourage mould to grow during storage. For chutneys, pickles and other preserves with vinegar, make sure the seals used are non-corrosive.

### STORAGE

Don't forget to label your preserve jars and bottles with its contents and the date it was made. Keep in a cool, dry, dark place in order to preserve colour and quality. If perfectly prepared and stored, most jams, jellies and marmalades will keep for up to 12 months; chutneys, pickles and vinegars for around six to eight months, and fruit cheeses up to six months. See specific recipes for other storage instructions.

# Freezing

Without doubt, freezing is the best way to preserve fruit and vegetables. Most produce will keep for up to 12 months in the freezer, giving you year round enjoyment – particularly good if you have a glut of produce. Choose only top quality, ripe, fresh produce for freezing – although slightly over-ripe fruit can be frozen in purée form. Specific instructions for individual fruit and vegetables are given in the glossary section of this book, but here are some general instructions.

## PREPARATION

Rinse unpeeled fruit and vegetables well and remove leaves and stalks as necessary.

## BLANCHING

The process by which vegetables are plunged into boiling water and, after the water comes back to boiling, are boiled for a short period of time. This inactivates enzymes, which would otherwise make the food deteriorate, and helps to retain vitamin C. Once the recommended boiling period is up, plunge the vegetables into iced water to cool as soon as possible, or place under running cold water. Pat dry thoroughly using kitchen paper in order to prevent too much ice forming during freezing and individual pieces sticking together in a solid lump.

## OPEN FREEZING

Particularly good for berries or prepared pieces of fruit and vegetable. Lay on trays lined with baking parchment and place in the freezer until solid. Either seal in freezer bags trying to expel as much air out of the bag as possible, or pack in rigid containers with fitted lids. Label and store until required. Freezing produce in this way will enable you to take out small measures from the bag at a time because the fruit shouldn't stick together once frozen and packed.

## PURÉED AND COOKED

Raw, ripe fruit such as berries and peaches can be puréed and packed into small rigid containers to freeze. If smaller quantities are required, freeze in ice cube trays and then transfer to freezer bags – you can then defrost small amounts as required. Fruit purée that discolours such as banana should be mixed with a little lemon juice or sugar to prevent browning. Purée is excellent for making sauces for ice cream, fruit coulis, and fruit fools. Cooked fruit can also be puréed down and frozen in the same way – stewed apples, plums and compotes freeze well in a purée.

## FREEZING FRUIT IN SUGAR

Use approximately 75–125 g (2½–4½ oz) caster sugar per 450 g (1 lb) fruit depending on how sweet the fruit is. As you layer the prepared fruit in its container, sprinkle lightly with sugar. On defrosting, the sugar will make its own juice. This is a good way to preserve a mixture of berries as once they defrost you have a readymade compote or topping for a cheesecake.

## FREEZING FRUIT IN SUGAR SYRUP

Some fruits discolour easily, for example peaches and apricots, and so a sugar syrup with added lemon juice is useful in order to prevent this. Dissolve 450 g (1 lb) caster sugar in 600 ml (1 pint) water and allow to cool completely. Stir in 2 tablespoons of lemon juice. Pack the prepared fruit into rigid freezer containers and pour over the syrup. Place a piece of baking parchment directly on top of the fruit in order to keep the fruit pieces submerged before you put the lid on. Label and store until required.

# USEFUL ADDRESSES

**SEED MERCHANTS/
PLANT SUPPLIERS/
GARDEN CENTRES**

**Chiltern seeds**
www.chilternseeds.co.uk

**Dobbies Garden
Centres plc**
www.dobbies.com

**Samuel Dobie and Sons**
www.dobies.co.uk

**Edwin Tucker and
Sons Ltd**
www.edwintucker.co.uk

**SEED MERCHANTS**
**Mr Fothergill's Seeds Ltd**
www.fothergills.co.uk

**Hillier Garden
Centres/Nurseries Ltd**
www.hillier.co.uk

**E W King and Co Ltd**
www.kingsseeds.co.uk

**Notcutts Garden
Centres**
www.notcutts.co.uk

**Sutton Seeds**
www.sutton-seeds.co.uk

**ASSOCIATIONS AND
ORGANISATIONS**

**The Allotments
Regeneration
Initiative**
A collaborative project
involving several organisations aiming to increase
the uptake of allotments.
www.farmgarden.org.uk/ari

**Henry Doubleday
Research Association
(HDRA)**
Heritage seed library and
catalogue; research and
promotion of organic
gardening and produce.
www.hdra.org.uk

**National Allotment
and Leisure Garden
Society (NSALG)**
www.nsalg.org.uk

**National Allotment
Gardens Trust**
A charitable organisation
aiming to promote
allotment gardening to
improve education and
public welfare.
www.nagtrust.org

**The Royal
Horticultural Society**
www.rhs.org.uk

**Scottish Allotment
and Garden Society**
www.sags.org.uk

**The Soil Association**
Main charity campaigning
for organic food and
farming.
www.soilassociation.org.uk

**KITCHEN EQUIP-
MENT SUPPLIERS**
**Cucina Direct**
www.cucinadirect.co.uk

**Lakeland Limited**
www.lakelandlimited.co.uk

**Style Cook Shop**
www.stylecookshop.co.uk

# ACKNOWLEDGEMENTS

I would like to thank friends and family who helped me out with tips, recipes, testing and tasting along the way, with a special thanks to my mum, Margaret, for all her hard work. Also, to Stella and Ian for the lovely photographs.

# BIBLIOGRAPHY

Berry, Mary **The Complete Book of Freezer Cooking** (Octopus, 1975)
Elliot, Rose **Vegetarian Cookery** (Harper Collins, 1992)
Foley, Caroline **The Allotment Handbook** (New Holland, 2004)
Foley, Caroline **The A–Z of Allotment Vegetables** (New Holland, 2006)
**Food from your Garden** (Reader's Digest, 1977)
**Larousse Gastronomique** (Paul Hamlyn, 1989)
Patten, Marguerite **Jams, Chutneys, Preserves, Vinegars and Oils** (Bloomsbury, 1995)
**The Cookery Year** (Reader's Digest, 1974)
Walden, Hilaire **Perfect Preserves** (Gary Allen, 2002)

# INDEX